WADSWORTH PHILOSC

On

KRISHNAMURTI

Raymond Martin
University of Maryland

THOMSON

™

WADSWORTH

Australia • Canada • Mexico • Singapore • Spain • United Kingdom • United States

For more information about our
products, contact us at:
Thomson Learning Academic
Resource Center
1-800-423-0563

For permission to use material from
this text, contact us by:
Phone: 1-800-730-2214
Fax: 1-800-731-2215
Web: www.thomsonrights.com

Asia
Thomson Learning
5 Shenton Way #01-01
UIC Building
Singapore 068808

Australia
Nelson Thomson Learning
102 Dodds Street
South Street
South Melbourne, Victoria 3205
Australia

Canada
Nelson Thomson Learning
1120 Birchmount Road
Toronto, Ontario M1K 5G4
Canada

Europe/Middle East/South Africa
Thomson Learning
High Holborn House
50-51 Bedford Row
London WC1R 4LR
United Kingdom

Latin America
Thomson Learning
Seneca, 53
Colonia Polanco
11560 Mexico D.F.
Mexico

Spain
Paraninfo Thomson Learning
Calle/Magallanes, 25
28015 Madrid, Spain

To

Dorothy

with love

Contents

Preface

Jiddhu Krishnamurti (1895-1986) was one of the 20th century's most highly visible and widely respected spiritual teachers. He had—and still has—an enormous following, East and West. In addition to being a spiritual teacher, he was a well-spring of philosophically significant insights, particularly on the phenomenology of self. The present book is an examination of his philosophy. It is the first book about his philosophy to be written by an analytic philosopher.

Virtually all of the quotations from Krishnamurti that occur in this book are from transcriptions that someone else made of talks or interviews that he gave. Few were written by Krishnamurti himself. The talks and interviews were given between the years 1933 and 1986. They almost always included question and answer sessions, which also have been transcribed. Throughout these years there is little, if any, change in his views, except what was occasioned by his responding to new questions that had not been asked previously. In other words, he had pretty much the same message from the beginning of this period to the end. In the case of some topics, he seems to have figured out along the way how to explain himself better. And the sorts of questions that people asked him changed somewhat with the times. But his message was consistent. As a consequence I have felt free to treat his entire recorded corpus during these years as if it were a single source.

Some of Krishnamurti's remarks in the present book are unpublished. Most have been published many times, in a variety of books and other publications, but often unpublished until many years (sometimes even decades) after the remarks were originally made. So, for the sake of simplicity, and also to increase the relevant information, I've identified what I've quoted from him on the basis of the dates of the talks or interviews from which the quoted remarks are taken; so, for instance, "(6 Sept 56)," after quoted remarks means that the remarks are taken from a talk or interview given by Krishnamurti on the 6th of September, 1956. All but one of the quotations in this book may be found on a CD-ROM which has been produced by the Krishnamurti Foundation Trust, and which includes information on the original published source. I am grateful to Mark Lee and Stephen Smith for allowing me to borrow this CD-ROM while I was writing this book. For permission to quote from Krishnamurti's works, I am grateful to the Krishnamurti Foundation of America, of Ojai, California, and to the Krishnamurti Foundation Trust, of Brockwood Park, Brandean, Hampshire, England. Between them they own all of the relevant copyrights.

Since the quotations from Krishnamurti that I have used are from transcriptions that someone else made of his remarks, it has been various editors, not Krishnamurti, who added punctuation and paragraph divisions to what originally was simply an oral presentation. So, in quoting, I have felt free to change the punctuation or to ignore paragraph divisions when it seemed more natural to do so. I have also changed British to American spelling: *centre* to *center*, *colour* to *color*, and so on.

Finally, many thanks to Chauncey Maher and to Stephen Smith for helpful remarks on an earlier draft of this book. Thanks also to Daniel Kolak, my friend, former student, and the general editor of this series, for deciding to include a book on Krishnamurti in the series. He knows, better than most, that although Krishnamurti is renowned outside the academy, he is not well known among academic philosophers. I think that Dan deserves credit for deciding to include in his series a book on Krishnamurti.

1
Introduction

Krishnamurti was not a philosopher in the usual sense. He did not study philosophy. He went out of his way to discourage people from regarding what he had to say as a contribution to philosophy. He did not try to clarify what he said in the ways that philosophers–at least academic ones–try to clarify what they say. And he never argued for his views.

Yet, Krishnamurti did have views–often original and insightful views–on many questions of philosophical concern. He expressed his views repeatedly over a period of more than thirty years. In keeping with the objectives of the Wadsworth Philosophers Series, in the present book my primary goal will be to trace the main contours of Krishnamurti's philosophical views. In doing this, I shall focus on what he had to say about the self–a topic that is central to his thought.

Instead of encouraging people to take what he had to say as a contribution to philosophy, Krishnamurti urged them to take it as an invitation to meditation. For him, meditation did not mean retreating from one's ordinary life–say, going off to a quiet spot to watch one's breath. Instead, it meant being extremely sensitive, without thought or external motive, to whatever in one's normal environment one is experiencing or doing in the moment. He was adamant on the importance of the difference between what is often taken to be meditation and the sort of meditation that he recommended:

This is meditation, real meditation, not all the phoney stuff. To see whether the mind–with the brain which has evolved

1

through time, which is the result of thousands of experiences, the brain that functions efficiently only in complete security—whether the mind can empty itself and yet have a brain that functions as a marvelous machine (26 Mar 71).

He regarded meditation in this sense as a technique for bypassing acquired conceptions— "images"—that keep one from seeing the truth:

So it is very important to understand that the act of seeing [that is, meditation] is the only truth; there is nothing else. If I know how to see a tree, or a bird, or a lovely face, or the smile of a child—there it is. I don't have to do anything more. But that seeing of the bird, or the leaf, listening to the noise of birds, becomes almost impossible because of the image that one has built, not only about nature but also about others. And these images actually prevent us from seeing and feeling
(3 Jan 68).

Meditation, then, in Krishnamurti's sense of the term, is seeing and feeling, in his senses of the terms.

In trying to understand the relationship between Krishnamurti's thought and the sort of philosophy that is ordinarily studied at the university, it is crucial to remember that in his view, it is meditation, not thought, that is the vehicle to those truths about ourselves that we most need to know. He conceded, of course, that thought is a vehicle to many other truths—in science and technology, for instance. But, in his view, thought is not meditation and it does not reveal the truths about ourselves that we most need to know. He said, for instance, "Even when we are sharpened and quickened intellectually by argument, by discussion, by reading, this does not actually bring about that quality of sensitivity. And you know, all those people who are erudite, who read, who theorize, who can discuss brilliantly, are extraordinarily dull people" (14 Jan 68). In other words, in his view, it's quite common for people who are brilliant theoretically to be insensitive when it comes to seeing and feeling, and hence blind to vital dimensions of themselves and their own activities.

Nevertheless, although meditating and theorizing are very different skills, they are both ways of trying to discover truths about the same world. So, *prima facie* there seems to be no reason why meditating and theorizing could not lead to complementary insights. Yet, these days academic philosophers tend to be dismissive of meditative attempts to understand self and world, and meditators, though to a lesser degree, tend to be dismissive of academic philosophy. I find both approaches

2

illuminating, so am interested in understanding this antagonism. In the present book, I would like to make a contribution to figuring out whether meditators and philosophers have anything to say to each other, particularly when they are both focused on the same issue, such as the nature of the self. So, in addition to my primary objective of tracing the main contours of Krishnamurti's philosophy, my secondary objective will be to use his thought as a vehicle for trying to understand whether meditation and philosophy are inherently antagonistic or potentially complementary. His thought is nearly ideal for this purpose. He dismissed philosophy. Yet, insofar as his unintentional theorizing was philosophically insightful, he contributed to it.

In sum, Krishnamurti was a curious blend of "spiritual" guide and philosopher. As guide, he facilitated meditation and pointed the way toward what, in his view, needs to be examined. As philosopher, he reported on what he took himself to have discovered through meditation, not in order to make a contribution to theory or to get anyone to accept his views, but to encourage others in their own individual processes of discovery. In both of these roles, he had a great deal to say about the human condition and especially about the self, which he regarded as a central topic of concern. He said, for instance, "The door is the 'me' through which I have to go. It is not outside of 'me.' It is not a factual door as that painted door. It is a door in me through which I have to go" (25 July 69).

My project of trying to understand the relationship between meditation and academic philosophy probably would not have interested Krishnamurti. He was focused on what he took to be the incomparably more important task of facilitating personal and social transformation. In his view, radical personal transformation, which he took to be essential if people are to live in the best way, must precede meaningful social transformation, which is essential if the world is to be saved from its own self-destructive tendencies. Radical personal transformation, he said, requires an inner revolution that cannot be brought about by thought. But even if Krishnamurti was right about this, it is still possible that thought (theorizing) can contribute to understanding the ways in which thought is an obstacle. Presumably his own thought was supposed to play this role. Even so, since he advocated meditating and had little use for philosophy, why a book about his philosophy?

The answer to that good question has two parts. First, even though Krishnamurti disdained theorizing, he theorized in spite of himself–quite a bit in fact; and in theorizing, he had important, original things to say about issues of philosophical concern. For instance, he had interesting and original things to say about the role of the psychological process of identification in self-constitution–a topic that had been discussed historically by such thinkers such as John Locke, David Hume, and William James. It is also a topic that is being discussed currently by various philosophers concerned with personal identity and the question of what matters in survival.[1] Second, and more importantly, quite apart from whatever unintentional contributions Krishnamurti may have made to philosophy, his message–about the need for personal and social transformation–may be, as he thought it was, among the most important issues that human beings need to consider.

Since Krishnamurti was not interested in philosophizing, but was interested in facilitating personal transformation it would be natural for someone who had never read his works to assume that he must have been interested in "self-improvement," and hence been a writer of self-help books. He was not. Although he had a rather dark view of the human condition–for instance, he believed that virtually everybody is in deep bondage to internal psychological conflicts that poison human experience and behavior–and dedicated his life to helping people to free themselves from what binds and blinds them, he was resolutely opposed to self-improvement programs. His opposition was not just to this or that program, but to the very idea that it might be a good thing for anyone to try to make him or herself into a better person. He claimed that one's trying to make oneself into a better person would not make one better, but more conflicted.

Krishnamurti claimed that what could make one into a better person–in fact, the only thing that would help–is learning certain deep truths about oneself and one's relationship to other people and the world. However, he thought that for this learning to have transformative power, one could not be told these truths, but must discover them for oneself, and that the discovery must be by "seeing" the truths, not thinking them. Since he believed that only in this way is revolutionary individual and social change possible, and that only on the basis of such change can the world survive as a habitat for people, ultimately he talked and wrote as if his goal were to save the world.

Notes

1. An elementary introduction to the philosophical problems of personal identity and of what matters in survival may be found in John Perry, *A Dialogue on Personal Identity and Immortality* (Indianapolis: Hackett, 1978). More sophisticated introductions may be found in Bernard Williams, "The Self and the Future," *Philosophical Review*, 79(1970)161-80, and Derek Parfit, "Personal Identity," *The Philosophical Review*, 80(1971)3-27. Useful anthologies include: Amelié Rorty, ed., *The Identities of Persons* (Berkeley: University of California Press,1976); John Perry, ed., *Personal Identity* (Berkeley: University of California Press, 1978); Daniel Kolak and Raymond Martin, eds., *Self & Identity: Contemporary Philosophical Issues* (New York: Macmillan, 1991); Raymond Martin and John Barresi, eds., *Personal Identity and What Matters in Survival* (Oxford: Blackwell, 2002). A selection of Krishnamurti's remarks that are particularly relevant to these issues may be found in Raymond Martin, ed., *J. Krishnamurti: Reflections on the Self*, Chicago: Open Court, 1997. Finally, for a philosophical theory of what matters in survival that drew inspiration from Krishnamurti's reflections, see Raymond Martin, *Self-Concern: An Experiential Approach to What Matters in Survival* (New York: Cambridge University Press, 1998).

2

Reluctant Messiah

Krishnamurti was born on May 12, 1895, in Madanapalle, India. He died, almost 91 years later, on February 18, 1986, in Ojai, California. Between his obscure birth and his widely-reported death, he led a remarkable–even fantastic–life. The decisive event that propelled him onto the world stage happened early. As a young boy the Theosophical Society thrust him into the role of messiah. The Society then spent a long time prepared him for this role, including educating him in England and France. In the end, dramatically, he turned down the part. But he turned it down not necessarily because he doubted that he was a messiah–apparently he thought that he was one–but because he believed that people are better off not relying on messiahs. What people need, he claimed, is not to be told the truth, but to discover it for themselves. And in this process, authorities, he said, have no place whatsoever.

Krishnamurti's parents had eleven children. He was the eighth. His mother, a devoutly religious woman, had a reputation for being psychic. It is said that she was so taken with the idea that her eighth child was to be special that she insisted, over the objections of her husband, that purity rituals be ignored and that the child be born in the puja room of their tiny house. The baby was named "Krishnamurti"–Krishna incarnate (according to Hindu legend, the god Sri Krishna was also an eighth child). The next day, as was (and is) the custom in India, a local astrologer was consulted. He predicted that Krishnamurti would be a great teacher, but only after surmounting serious obstacles.

Krishnamurti's father graduated from Madras University and went to work for the British Department of Revenue. His mother ran a traditional Brahmin home. When Krishnamurti was ten years old, she died. Two years later his father was forced to retire from the British Administration on a meager pension. He joined the Theosophical Society. Two years later he secured a job with the Society. In exchange for work, he and four of his sons, including Krishnamurti and his younger brother Nityananda (Nitya), were accommodated in a cottage outside the 260 acre Theosophical Society Compound in Adyar, near Madras.

The Theosophical Society had been founded in New York, thirty-four years earlier, by Madame Blavatsky and Colonel Olcott. Blavatsky claimed to have lived in Tibet and to have learned occult wisdom from "the Masters"–supposedly perfected human beings who periodically appeared on Earth to found a new religion and to direct the course of human evolution. In 1882, Blavatsky and Olcott purchased the estate at Adyar for the Society's headquarters. Seven years later, Annie Besant, a political radical and friend of George Bernard Shaw, joined the Society. In the following year, she met and befriended Charles Leadbeater, a former priest in the Church of England. After the deaths of Blavatsky and Olcott, and two years prior to Krishnamurti's arrival at the Compound, Besant became president of the Society. She and Leadbeater were in residence when Krishnamurti arrived.

Central to Theosophy is the teaching that humans are progressively evolving toward universal brotherhood. On the way to this end, seven root-races are to appear sequentially, at the origin of each of which a world-teacher will incarnate to impart a spiritual message. When Krishnamurti arrived at the Theosophical Society Compound members of the sect were expecting the appearance of a world teacher–Maitreya. They believed that Maitreya was going to incarnate as a boy. They hoped to find this boy and then to raise and train him.

For years prior to Krishnamurti's arrival at the Compound, Leadbeater, who was thought to be remarkably psychic, and Besant had been collaborating in occult investigations, which according to them often included astral travel to meet with the Masters. In the summer of 1909, while on a walk outside the Compound, Leadbeater spied Krishnamurti, who was then thirteen years old. He wrote that he was so overwhelmed by what he took to be Krishnamurti's extraordinary aura that he became convinced that Krishnamurti was destined to be a great spiritual teacher.

Leadbeater then began to investigate what he took to be Krishnamurti's past lives–forty-eight of them. Believing himself to have discovered that previously Krishnamurti had been Alcyone, he reported

7

in the *Theosophist* on Krishnamurti's lives as Alcyone. As these reports were being publicized, the leadership of the Theosophical Society–though not without dissent–determined to its own satisfaction that Krishnamurti was to be the physical vehicle for Maitreya. One of the dissenters was Rudolph Steiner, who at the time was a Theosophist. Unhappy with the decision, or with the way it was made, he resigned from the Society and formed his own society, which he called *Anthroposophy*. Regardless, once the Theosophical Society leadership had decided that Krishnamurti was to be the new vehicle for the World Teacher, he and his brother Nitya were brought into the Compound, attended to physically, and given lessons.

In addition to ordinary schoolwork, Krishnamurti's lessons included daily astral trips, guided by Leadbeater, to meet with the Master Kuthumi.[1] Reportedly, in January, 1910, after five months of these lessons, Krishnamurti, in astral form, was initiated by Kuthumi for his role as vehicle for the World Teacher. Supposedly present at this ceremony were Maitreya, Buddha (Siddhartha Gautama), Besant, and Leadbeater. The next year, within the Theosophical Society, an organization was formed which became the Order of the Star in the East. Its purpose was to herald the arrival of the new World Teacher: Krishnamurti.

For the next ten years, Krishnamurti and Nitya were educated in England, where Krishnamurti became close to Lady Emily Lutyens, whom he regarded as his foster mother. Through her, he lived as an English aristocrat, exercising at Sandow's gymnasium, attending ballet, opera, film, theater, and the races, and visiting art galleries. He traveled extensively. During this time he is said to have become a scratch golfer and to have learned how to take apart an automobile engine and put it back together. He also read widely, including works of Stephen Leacock, P.G. Wodehouse, Turgenev, Dostoevsky, Nietzsche, Bergson, Shelley, and Keats. He was particularly impressed by Paul Carus' *The Buddha's Way of Virtue, The Gospel According to the Buddha*, from which he copied for Lady Emily the passage, "All conquering and all knowing am I, detached, untainted, untrammeled, wholly freed by destruction of desire. Whom shall I call Teacher? Myself found the way."

In 1921, Krishnamurti went to Paris where he took courses at the Sorbonne and studied Sanskrit. While there, he began to write editorial notes in a quarterly magazine for members of the Order of the Star. Then, during a visit to Holland from Paris, he met and fell in love with Helen Knothe, a young American girl who had gone to Holland to study music. Because of the obligation that he felt to his role as vehicle for the World

Teacher his attachment to her left him deeply conflicted. With great reluctance, he left her. The next year he and Nitya moved to Ojai, California, where, it was hoped, the dry climate would help Nitya in his battle with tuberculosis.

During the summer of 1922, in Ojai, after several weeks of sustained meditation, Krishnamurti had a life-transforming experience. He described it as follows: "There was a man mending the road; that man was myself; the pickaxe he held was myself; the very stone he was breaking up was a part of me; the tender blade of grass was my very being, and the tree beside the man was myself." The next day, while sitting under a nearby pepper tree, Krishnamurti had a second extraordinary experience, after which he wrote, "I was supremely happy, for I had seen. Nothing could ever be the same." He wrote, "I had touched compassion which heals all sorrow and suffering," and that it was not for himself, "but for the world":

> *I have stood on the mountain top and gazed at the mighty Beings. Never can I be in utter darkness; I have seen the glorious and healing Light. The fountain of Truth has been revealed to me and the darkness has been dispersed. Love in all its glory has intoxicated my heart; my heart can never be closed. I have drunk at the fountain of Joy and eternal Beauty.*[2]

Krishnamurti wrote that he was "God-intoxicated."

In November of 1925, Nitya died and Krishnamurti experienced the most profound grief of his life. On an ocean voyage when he received the news, he confined himself to his cabin where he cried profusely for several days. Reportedly, however, by the time he arrived at land he was calm and cheerful, with no visible signs of strain.

During the next few years, Krishnamurti began to distance himself from Theosophy and to develop some of the distinctive motifs of his own subsequent teachings. The decisive break with Theosophy came in August, of 1929. In the presence of 3000 members of the Society, he dissolved the Order of the Star, proclaiming:

> *I maintain that Truth is a pathless land, and you cannot approach it by any path whatsoever, by any religion, by any sect. That is my point of view, and I adhere to it absolutely and unconditionally. Truth, being limitless, unconditioned, unapproachable by any path whatsoever, cannot be organized; nor should any organization be formed to lead or coerce people along any particular path.*

He told his audience, "You will probably form other Orders, you will continue to belong to other organizations searching for Truth." But, he said, "If an organization be created for this purpose, it becomes a crutch, a weakness, a bondage, and must cripple the individual, and prevent him from growing, from establishing his uniqueness, which lies in the discovery for himself of that absolute, unconditioned Truth." He continued, "Because I am free, unconditioned, whole, not the part, not the relative, but the whole Truth that is eternal, I desire those, who seek to understand me, to be free, not to follow me, not to make out of me a cage which will become a religion, a sect." He concluded, "I have now decided to disband the Order, as I happen to be its Head. You can form other organizations and expect someone else. With that I am not concerned, nor with creating new cages, new decorations for those cages. My only concern is to set men absolutely, unconditionally free."[3]

The next year, in 1930, Krishnamurti formally resigned from the Theosophical Society and returned to Ojai to meditate and to think. During this time he wrote to Lady Emily that he had understood and conquered "sorrow, this pain of detachment and attachment, death, continuity of life, everything that man goes through, everyday." He wrote, "I know the way out of this incessant misery, and I want to help people out." Later he wrote, "You have no idea how difficult it is to express the inexpressible and what is expressed is not truth."[4]

From 1933 to 1939, Krishnamurti traveled extensively, talking to large audiences. From 1941 to 1945, forbidden to travel, he led a life of relative seclusion at Ojai. During this time he became close friends with Aldous Huxley, who encouraged him to write. After the War, Krishnamurti resumed his traveling and talking, which he continued until he died. On average, he gave about 175 talks a year, often to audiences of several thousand. In addition, he had personal and small-group discussions with many who came to see him. On one lighthearted occasion, in California, he went on a picnic with Bertrand Russell, Charlie Chaplin, Greta Garbo, Aldous Huxley, and Christopher Isherwood. The group got into trouble with a local sheriff for trespassing and had to move the picnic from the coast to Huxley's backyard.

In 1953, Krishnamurti wrote *Education and the Significance of Life*. The next year he wrote, *The First and Last Freedom*, which included a foreword by Huxley. Then there appeared three volumes entitled, *Commentaries on Living*. Subsequently he wrote or spoke the text for three books: *Krishnamurti's Notebook*, a personal journal, recorded mostly in 1961; *Krishnamurti's Journal*, from writings he had done in 1973 and 1975; and *Krishnamurti to Himself*, his last journal, made from comments which he spoke into a tape recorder. His many other books, which number over 40, are edited transcriptions of talks and discussions held by him in various parts of the world. Usually he talked with everyday people. But he also talked with many famous people, including John Barrymore, who offered him a role in a movie playing the Buddha (Krishnamurti declined), Joseph Campbell, Leopold Stokowski, the Nobel laureates Maurice Wilkins and Jonas Salk, the theoretical physicist David Bohm, and the Buddhist scholar Walpola Rahula. Videotapes of many of these discussions are available, and excerpts from them are included in several films that have been made about Krishnamurti.

Notes

1. The teachings that Krishnamurti reportedly received from Kuthumi are recorded in a book, *At the Feet of the Master*, by Alcyone. This book, which is still in print, has been translated into twenty-seven languages and has gone through forty editions.

2. Mary Lutyens, *Krishnamurti:The Years of Awakening* (New York: Farrar, Straus, & Giroux, 1975), pp. 170-72.

3. *The Dissolution of the Order of the Star*, 3 August 1929. Quoted in Mary Lutyens, *Krishnamurti:The Years of Awakening* , pp.272-75.

4. Mary Lutyens, *Krishnamurti:The Years of Awakening,* p. 281.

3

Inquiry

There is no privileged place to begin a consideration of Krishnamurti's thought–no one issue around which everything else resolves. Or, if there is, there are many different ways of approaching it. Encountering his thought for the first time can be like coming by accident upon an ongoing conversation. Overheard words momentarily capture your attention, and you listen. Words such as these, perhaps:

> *Because you have placed beliefs before life, creeds before life, dogmas before life, religions before life, there is stagnation. Can you bind the waters of the sea or gather the winds in your fist? Religion, as I understand it, is the frozen thought of men out of which they have built temples and churches. The moment you attribute to external authority a spiritual and divine law and order, you are limiting, you are suffocating, that very life that you wish to fulfill, to which you would give freedom. If there is limitation, there is bondage and hence suffering. The world at present is the expression of life in bondage. So, according to my point of view, beliefs, religions, dogmas, and creeds, have nothing to do with life, and hence have nothing to do with truth.*[1]

Or these words:

If you have ever inquired very deeply into yourself, you are bound to have come upon that state which we call loneliness, a sense of complete isolation, of not being related. As a human being, you must at some time have felt that desperate, agonizing, despairing sense of isolation, from which consciously or unconsciously we are always running away. In our flight from the reality of that extraordinary sense of loneliness, we are driven, are we not, by a deep urge that is everlastingly seeking fulfillment through books, through music, through work and activity, through position, power, prestige (11 Mar 59).

In such remarks, Krishnamurti expressed his views about the relationship between creeds and life, about the relationship between words and reality, and about how people respond to what they discover when they look into their own minds. But, as he repeatedly reminded his audiences, he did not want them to listen in order to learn his views, but to inquire along with him. And he did not want them, even in a critical frame of mind, to consider what he said merely intellectually. Rather, he wanted them to look inside themselves–for instance, to encounter the loneliness inside themselves and to observe their reaction to it. From his point of view, the worst response that people could make to hearing or reading what he had to say would be for them to accept it because he said it.

So, having overheard such remarks, your reaction may be that what Krishnamurti said is boring, shallow, or even repellant, in which case you might turn away. Alternatively, you may feel yourself being drawn into the "conversation," in which case you might listen more fully. If that were to happen, you would soon discover that the man whose words you overheard made a practice of talking passionately and intelligently about important human concerns. He may have been right or wrong in what he said, but he did not talk casually. When he addressed a topic, he picked one that he thought was important to human well being, and he tried to get to the heart of the matter.

Did Krishnamurti often succeed in getting to the heart of the matter? You decide. What he said is so different from what just about everybody else has said, and is saying, that it is difficult to assess it by the same criteria. And not only is his message different, but he himself seems to be different. For one thing, he is remarkably calm, and yet there is urgency in his voice. For another, in his manner and what he is saying, there is no hint of self-promotion. Finally, although he spoke with so much authority, he was adamant about not being an authority.

Naturally, Krishnamurti told his audiences things that he believed (how could he not?). Yet, he was intent on trying not to feed them beliefs.

Typical, for instance, are these remarks:

> *A lecture generally means telling or explaining a certain subject, for you to be instructed, to learn. This is not a lecture. Here, we are having a conversation together like two friends . . . because we are concerned, both you and the speaker, with our daily life, not with something beyond, romantic and fantastic. . . . Please, if one may point out, it is your responsibility to think together, not to accept, because one must have a great deal of skepticism, a skepticism that is not trammeled by fear, a doubt so that one begins to question not only what the speaker is saying but also what you think, what you believe, your faith, your conclusions, your religion. One must have tremendous questioning, doubt, inquiry, through deep exploration, not accepting, . . . We are together going to look at many things that confront our daily life. we are not going to talk about any philosophy, any dogma, or encourage any faith, but with a mind that is questioning, doubting, demanding, find out for ourselves what is true, what is illusory, what is fantastic, and what is false* (29 Jan 83).

In sum, Krishnamurti had a view about how learning takes place, at least learning the sorts of things with which he was most concerned. And the heart of his approach was not to accept, but to question. In short, he encouraged skepticism–about everything.

In Krishnamurti's view, you never learn the things about yourself that you most need to know by being told, or even by reflecting intellectually, and then judging what you have heard against the backdrop of other things that you believe or think you know.

> *Are we taking a journey together ? Or are you merely following? It is for you to tell me, not for me to tell you. . . . Are we journeying together or are you being led–which is it? If you are being led, if you are following, there is no relationship, because the speaker says, "Don't follow." He is neither your authority nor your guru; if you insist on following, if you insist on listening in order to learn what he is saying, then there is no relationship. But if you say, "I want to learn," [then] we are taking a journey together into the extraordinary world in which we live . . .* (20 July 71).

So, instead of providing those who came to hear him with another belief to add to their stock of beliefs, Krishnamurti was inviting them to engage with him in a cooperative enterprise–a dialogue–in which he and they addressed the same fundamental issues, at the same time, with the same passionate intensity.

The goal of this mutual activity is not to provide people with another theory, not even if they thought it up for themselves. The goal, rather is to see whether it is possible to live without accumulating beliefs. Thus, he said, for instance:

> *If I am merely a repeating machine, as most of us are–repeating what we have learned, what we have gathered, passing on what has been told to us–then any thought arising within this conditioned field obviously can only lead to further conditioning, further misery and limitation. So, can the mind, knowing its limitation, being aware of its conditioning, go beyond itself? That is the problem. Merely to assert that it can, or it cannot, would be silly. Surely it is fairly obvious that the whole mind is conditioned. We are all conditioned–by tradition, by family, by experience, through the process of time. If you believe in God, that belief is the outcome of particular conditions, just as is the disbelief of the man who says he does not believe in God. So belief and disbelief have very little importance. But what is important is to understand the whole field of thought, and to see if the mind can go beyond it all* (6 Sept 56).

And this:

> *The moment the guru says he knows, then you may be sure he doesn't know. Because what he knows is something past, obviously. Knowledge is the past. And when he says he knows, he is thinking of some experience which he has had, which he has been able to recognize as something great, and that recognition is born out of his previous knowledge, otherwise he couldn't recognize it, and therefore his experience has its roots in the past. Therefore it is not real* (26 Mar 71).

In other words, what Krishnamurti asked is whether the mind, which is conditioned to structure its experience on the basis of categories it has stored, and to think through the medium of theories it has learned and beliefs it has accumulated, can escape from all of this conditioning in a way that is conducive to discovering the truth. Can such a mind, he asked, do something radically different from what it is accustomed to doing, namely, can it bypass thought and connect directly to reality?

In Krishnamurti's view, the mind cannot connect directly to reality if it approaches reality through the medium of theories. Thinking, he said, is a material process, and as such it is conditioned. Even what we ordinarily call experience, "is not real experience, but only conditioned experience." It is conditioned experience because it is mediated by thought. The "right kind of experience," he said, is direct experience, which is not mediated by thought, and so not conditioned. Hence, one can experience directly "only when thinking ceases" (28 Dec 47). The point, he claimed, is not to acquire another belief, or another conditioned experience, but to connect directly to reality.

Most people listen, Krishnamurti continued, "to be told what to do, or to conform to a new pattern," or they listen "merely to gather further information." But, he said, if we listen in any of those frames of mind we will not learn, at least not in a way that could facilitate meaningful personal and social transformation. According to him, that sort of potentially transformative learning is undercut by wanting to be taught:

> *When you begin to inquire into the operation of your own mind, when you observe your own thinking, your daily activities and feelings, you cannot . . . base your inquiry on any authority, on any assumption, on any previous knowledge. If you do, then you are merely conforming to the pattern of what you already know, and therefore you are no longer learning about yourself* (20 Feb 57).

The point, rather, in his view, is to attend as fully and freshly as you can to your own current experience, learning as you go, but not gathering what you learn into a theory, even into one that you continually revise, and then using that theory as a lens though which to examine whatever is going on in the next moment. Instead of gathering your seeming (or genuine) insights into a theory, you simply allow what you learn to affect you, in whatever way it does, without trying to determine in advance what way that will be. He thought that the likely effect of proceeding in this way is that your freedom will be enhanced. However, he claimed, this effect, if it happens, will not come about as a consequence of your desire, or effort, to achieve it. 'It is truth that frees," he said, not your desire to be free and "not your effort to be free."

In such a process of learning, authority has no place. According to Krishnamurti, if you accept anything because someone has said it, or because it is written in a book that you admire, then you cannot inquire with an open mind. So, in his view, no teachers, no scripture, no theories, no faith of any kind, not even the authority of your own past experience, is going to help. Rather, in the sort of open-minded investigation that he recommended, you will learn, he thought, how relying on authority narrows and deadens the mind. In trying to understand something–life, your mind, whatever–directly, something that is alive and constantly changing, it does not help, he said, to view it through the lens of a theory, which in the nature of the case, is dead and static. He said that looking at what is alive and changing through something that is dead and static–looking at the new through the lens of the old–only obscures your view, preventing you from having a genuinely original insight. He claimed that it is better–more clarifying–to look without a filter.

Thus, Krishnamurti's approach, since it is based on seeing–a kind of observation–is scientific in the broad sense of the word. Yet it is contrary to the ways in which scientific investigation is generally conducted. Ordinarily, in a scientific context, one approaches nature not in an openly questioning, intellectually passive way, but with specific questions in mind that have been formulated in advance. In other words, one goes to Nature not passively, in order to learn whatever Nature wants to teach, but rather, aggressively, armed with a specific question and intent on forcing Nature to answer it. The answer, if it is forthcoming, is then not abandoned, but gathered up, recorded, and stored. It is then used to elaborate and test a theory.

So, one cannot follow Krishnamurti's approach and at the same time approach issues scientifically, in this traditional way. But that is the only way in which his approach is incompatible with science as ordinarily practiced. Otherwise, it is quite compatible. He was not against doing science, and in recommending the approach that he did, he was not recommending *a procedure for doing science*. Rather, he was recommending an approach to doing meditation.

Dialogue, in the sense in which Krishnamurti recommended the practice, is a communicative, meditative exercise in which two or more people talk to each other. In dialogue, verbal understanding is essential. But for genuine communication to take place, he claimed, listening openly is also essential. He said that to whatever extent in trying to listen, one's opinions, background, prejudices, inclinations, and so on intrude, listening is diminished. "One listens and therefore learns, only in a state of attention, a state of silence in which this whole background is in abeyance, is quiet. Then, it seems to me, it is possible to communicate." Listening in this way, thus, also means not projecting your ideas and images about the person with whom you are talking onto what he or she says. In sum, "When two people are intent, seriously, to understand something, bringing their whole mind and heart, their nerves, their eyes, their ears, to understand, then in that attention there is a certain quality of silence: then communication, actual communication, takes place" (19 Jan 52).

Krishnamurti encouraged his listeners to consider whether it is possible to inquire, and more generally to live, without relying for their understanding of themselves either on external authority or even the authority of their own theories. In his view, that is a key question. Of course, even if it were *possible* to live without relying on authority, it would be a separate question whether it would be a good thing to live that way.

Krishnamurti claimed that it would be a good thing to live that way. In his view, if it were not possible to live without relying on authority, it would not be possible for us to break free of the shackles of our own minds. But if, as he thought, the answer to the question of whether for our understanding of ourselves we can live without authority is, yes, then genuine inquiry becomes possible; and with genuine inquiry, real learning; and with real learning, freedom.

In genuine dialogue, Krishnamurti claimed, one must start close to home–that is, inquire about something that falls within your immediate purview. If you are going to rely only on your own current experience, and not on theories, then you have to start close to home. To illustrate what he had in mind, he put himself in the place of someone he imagined to be listening:

I am here, an ordinary human being. I have not read a thing. I want to know. Where am I to begin? I have to work: in a garden, as a cook, in a factory, in an office; I have to work. And also there are the wife and children: I love them, I hate them, I am a sexual addict because that is the only escape offered to me in life. Here I am. That is my map of life and I start from here. I cannot start from over there; I start here and I ask myself what it is all about. I know nothing about God. You can invent, pretend; I have a horror of pretending. If I do not know, I do not know. I am not going to quote . . . anybody (25 July 69).

And, on another occasion:

You see, I only start with what is a fact, for me. What is a fact, not according to some philosophers and religious teachers and priests, a fact: I suffer, I have fear, I have sexual demands. How am I to deal with all these tremendously complex things which make my life?–and I am so utterly miserable, unhappy. From there I start, not from what somebody said, that means nothing (23 June 78).

But in spite of one's beginning with oneself, genuine inquiry of this sort, he thought, is not self-centered. And this, for two reasons: first, we are all so much alike; and, second, social relations are a reflection of our inner confusion.

Out of the disorder of our own lives, Krishnamurti claimed, order can arise, not just for ourselves personally, but for everyone:

> *Disorder means conflict, acceptance of authority, complying, imitation, all that. That is disorder, the social morality is disorder. Out of that I will bring order in myself, not myself as a petty little human being in a backyard, but as a Human Being. Every human being is going through this hell. So if I as a human being, understand this, I have discovered something that all human beings can discover* (25 July 69).

And, thus, is the path made ready for real revolution:

> *What I am saying is very clear and simple if you will follow it. Society is your own product, it is your projection. The world's problem is your problem, and to understand that problem you have to understand yourself; and you can understand yourself only in relationship, not in escapes. Because you escape through them, your religion, your knowledge have no validity, no significance. You are unwilling to alter fundamentally your relationship with another because that means trouble, that means disturbance, revolution; so you talk about the highbrow intellectual, the mystic, and all the rest of that nonsense. A new society, a new order, cannot be established by another; it must be established by you. A revolution based on an idea is not a revolution at all. Real revolution comes from within, and that revolution is not brought about through escape, but comes only when you understand your relationships, your daily activities, the way you are acting, the way you are thinking, the way you are talking, your attitude to your neighbor, to your wife, to your husband, to your children. Without understanding yourself, whatever you do, however far you may escape will only produce more misery, more wars, more destruction (10 Jan 62).*

But for real revolution, people must enquire, not seek:

> *A mind that is enquiring–not seeking–must be totally free of these two, that is, of the demand for experience and the search for truth* (25 April 71).

Notes

1. *Life the Goal*, 1928. As quoted in Evelyne Blau, *Krishnamurti: 100 Years* (New York: Stewart, Tabori, & Chang, 1995), p. 76.

4
Self

What is the self? According to Krishnamurti, it is an experiential, or phenomenological, illusion, composed of what he called *images*. Unfortunately, he used the word *images* rather loosely. However, what he seems to have meant by it, in the present context, is an item, usually in experience, that has been *conceptualized* or *interpreted*.

In this interpretation is correct, then constructing an image results from conceptualizing or interpreting some previously unconceptualized mental element, presumably a signal that enters the mind from outside. In addition to this sort of image, Krishnamurti sometimes classified things in the world with which people "identified," such as their furniture, as images. However, he also talked about the necessity of "dissolving" images. So, when he called physical objects, like furniture, images, presumably what he meant is that their being "things" of the sort that we imagine them to be, instead of something more realistic, is the result of a mental contribution that the mind makes to their reification.

As we shall see, in Krishnamurti's way of talking about this process of conceptualization or interpretation, when one conceptualizes or interprets an external object or an element in the mind, "experience" results. Experience, thus, is composed of "images." The connection between images and the self is twofold: first, the self is composed of images; and, second, the self comes into being at least partly as a

22

Self

consequence of the construction of images–in experience. Typical, for instance, of the things Krishnamurti said about this process is that when "I construct" an image about something, "I am able to watch that image, so there is the image and the observer of the image."

Minimally, when Krishnamurti talked of constructing an image, he simply meant conceptualizing something. But often he meant something more elaborate–he meant thinking thoughts. One might think thoughts about something, for instance, by consciously remembering other occasions when one encountered the same thing or a similar thing, or by reviving feeling about that sort of thing. These ways of thinking thoughts about something are ways of interpreting an item in experience. Merely conceptualizing, without thinking such thoughts, may also be regarded as an act of interpretation, but compared to the acts of interpretation just mentioned it is minimally interpretive.

To get clearer about what it might mean to conceptualize something, suppose, for instance, that in looking at a tree, you think, *tree*–that is, you categorize, or recognize, the object that you are looking at *as a tree*. In that case, in looking visually at a tree, a signal (presumably light being reflected off the tree) has affected your mind, and you have conceptualized that signal (or the "object" which it represents)–as a *tree*. That sort of conceptualizing is a rather minimal way of interpreting such a signal (or object). A more robust way of interpreting it would first be to conceptualize it as *tree*, and then to think thoughts about it, such as, "Wouldn't it be lovely to have that tree in my front yard." In Krishnamurti's manner of speaking, both of these ways of interpreting the tree would be ways of forming *images*.

Ordinarily, when we look at something in the world, or in our own minds, there are layers and layers of conceptualizing and interpreting going on, of different sorts. In looking, for instance, at the woman who is your wife, you might think (or see her as) *woman* or, more robustly, you might think (or see her as) *wife.*[1] In conceptualizing your wife in either of these ways, you also might remember various pleasures or antagonisms that you associate with her. And you might also call to mind various theories that you have about her–for instance, "probably right now she's thinking of her mother; she always thinks of her mother on occasions like this." You might also have an evaluative reaction to her–I love her, I hate her, or whatever. In Krishnamurti's sense of *image*, each of these ways of *experiencing* your wife would involve constructing "images" of her. Some of these images would result from minimally conceptualizing her, others from more robustly conceptualizing her, others from thinking thoughts about her, others from feeling affect toward her, and so on.

In Krishnamurti's view, the self is composed exclusively of images. And these images, collectively, are illusory. What makes them illusory is that they seem to be a self, but are not one really. To be a genuine self, were there such a thing, the images would have to be an active agent–a *doer*. But the images that collectively constitute the self are merely passive–albeit transitory–items in the mind.

More specifically, the images that constitute the self are illusory in four ways: First, collectively they make it appear that one is aware in one's own experience of (and as) an "observer" who is distinct from what is observed when, in reality, "the observer" is merely images, and hence part of what is observed. Second, "the observer" appears to be an agent, or as Krishnamurti often said, a "center." What this means is that the observer appears to be a perceiver and evaluator (or, judge), and as such is contrasted with those images that constitute "the observed"–that is, those images which it seems mistakenly that "the observer" perceives and evaluates. Third, whereas the images that collectively constitute the self are transient, they seem to be permanent, or at least to have a permanent core: "This observer who has come into being through various other images thinks himself permanent and between himself and the images he has created there is a division."[2] Finally, between the observer and the observed there is something that Krishnamurti called *space*: "There is space which the center creates round itself, which is the space of isolation" (26 Mar 71).

According to Krishnamurti, as a consequence of the mind's images being apparently divided between observer and observed, when one looks at something–say, at one's wife–one looks *as if* from the perspective of an "observer": "It is from that center that I observe and make my judgment, and thus the observer is separate from the thing he observes." It is *as if* the observer is aware of many images, often at the same time, and is "always adding to and subtracting from" these, and to and from "what he is," by "weighing, comparing, judging, modifying and changing as a result of pressures from outside and within–living in the field of consciousness which is his own knowledge, influence and innumerable calculations."

At the same time when you look at the observer, who is yourself, you see that he is made up of memories, experiences, accidents, influences, traditions and infinite varieties of suffering, all of which are the past. So the observer is both the past and the present, and tomorrow is waiting and that is also a part of him. He is half alive and half dead and with this death and life he is looking, . . .[3]

In sum, the individual, *as if* through the lens of his images, which are constantly changing in various ways and for various reasons, but which always present themselves in experience as if they were an observer, observes other things which because he has already conceptualized or interpreted them, or is currently conceptualizing or interpreting them, are also images.

Krishnamurti often talked of the observer as something that "thinks." What he meant, I believe, is that the individual in whose mind there is this collection of "images"–this "self" or "observer"–thinks as if from the perspective of these images. In other words, what he was saying is that in the human mind there is a constantly changing constellation of images which seems to be–but is not actually– permanent, which seems to be–but is not actually–an *observer*, or *perceiver*, a thinker, an evaluator, and so on, and which seems to be–but is not actually–separate from the rest of the mind's contents–"the observed."

Krishnamurti said that this subtle illusion of a self in experience encourages the individual in whose mind it has taken root to evaluate, and subsequently to take action in regard to, those images that he or she takes to be "the observed." He said that this sort of motivation to take action, and the ensuing action, is a source of internal conflict:

> *One image, as the observer, observes dozens of other images around himself and inside himself, and he says, "I like this image, I'm going to keep it" or "I don't like that image so I'll get rid of it", but the observer himself has been put together by the various images which have come into being through reaction to various other images. So we come to a point where we can say, "the observer is also the image, only he has separated himself and observes." This observer who has come into being through various other images thinks himself permanent and between himself and the images he has created there is a division, a time interval. This creates conflict between himself and the images he believes to be the cause of his troubles. So then he says, "I must get rid of this conflict," but the very desire to get rid of the conflict creates another image.*[4]

In other words, when the self–the observer half of the observer/observed phenomenon–is a feature of peoples' experience, they become motivated in ways that they would not otherwise have become motivated to do something about the objects of their experience, or about the experiences themselves; for instance, they become motivated to try to make them stay or to make them go away. So, in Krishnamurti's view, the observer/observed distinction generates conflict within individuals who harbor the distinction. But if, knowing this, people should want to rid their experience of the observer/observed distinction, that very wanting would only strengthen the distinction and is itself an additional source of conflict.

As we have seen, Krishnamurti also said that the distinction between observer and observed shows up in experience as a kind of psychological "space." How is this notion to be understood? No doubt the *best* way to understand it would be to be aware of oneself or the external world without the observer/observed distinction being present in one's awareness, and hence without any psychological space between "observer" and "observed." One could then compare that sort of awareness with ordinary experience, in which there is both the observer/observed distinction and the space. Unfortunately one cannot just make this sort of undivided awareness happen.

Fortunately, there is, I think, an alternative way to understand the notion of psychological space. It is to reflect on those occasions when you have been aware without being "self-conscious." Remember, for instance, some time when you were so completely caught up in working on something–say, a math problem–that you had no sense of self. So far as your experience at such times is concerned, there was just the object of your experience–say, various thoughts that collectively constituted your working on the math problem. Such "no self experiences" are quite common. They may have occurred, for instance, when you were *completely* caught up in listening to music, or dancing, or having sex. People sometimes say that in experiences of these sorts they "lose themselves." That's exactly right. When the experiences in which they lose themselves begin, all of their self-consciousness, and with it their illusion of self, drops out of their experience. People also say things to indicate the lack of divisiveness in such experiences: for instance, "The dancer was the dance"; "We two were one"; and so on. At such times of mental unification, there may have been in their experience no psychological space between observer and observed. However, with the return of self-consciousness, the illusion of oneself as observer, and of what one was observing as the observed, reentered experience.

An interesting feature of our ordinary experiences in which there is no self-consciousness is that as soon as one introspects, the observer/observed distinction, and with it the psychological space, returns. The reason for this is that in the sort of common no-self experiences that we have been discussing, what collapses the sense of distance–the psychological space–is that one's attention is totally absorbed by some object or activity. Break the absorption, say, by introspecting, and the sense of space returns. However, in Krishnamurti's view, it is possible to be aware, even while introspecting, without self-consciousness, and without the psychological space that ordinarily attends self-consciousness.

In other words, in what, for want of a better label, we may call *uncommon no-self awareness,* concentration on, or absorption in, an object or activity is not necessary to keep the observer/observed phenomenon at bay. In that sort of awareness, one might even carefully introspect in search of an observer without the observer/observed phenomenon reappearing. That is, in that sort of awareness, it is not just that one introspectively looks for and then fails to find the observer/observed phenomenon. It is, rather, that the same sort of immediacy and lack of psychological space that is a feature of common no-self experiences is a feature even of one's relaxed introspective awareness.

For those familiar with the history of modern western philosophy, it may be useful at this point to compare Krishnamurti's view of the self with that of David Hume, the great 18th century British empiricist. Hume famously claimed that people, in examining the contents of their own experience, mistakenly interpret as a more or less constant self what is actually a succession of individual "perceptions"–what, in Hume's view, correspond to Krishnamurti's minimally conceptualized "images." These perceptions, Hume said, come and then go "with an inconceivable rapidity." In his view, it is resemblances among these perceptions, together with the fact that they come and go so rapidly, that creates the illusion of self. In other words, it is like the illusion of continuity that can be created when discontinuous images are flashed too quickly for normal perception to distinguish them as discrete and discontinuous, such as occurs when one watches a motion picture.

Hume said that "our propensity to this mistake," that is, to misinterpret transient perceptions for a relatively permanent self, is so ubiquitous and strong "that we fall into it before we are aware." He also said that even after we become aware of our error, we cannot help falling back into it. Even worse, he claimed, "in order to justify to ourselves this absurdity," we make up a story in which the principle character is self or soul, or substance, and once this story is in place, we hide in it. In short, in Hume's view, because of the way our experience presents itself in awareness, an illusion of permanence and internal agency emerges where neither is present, and then "we"–the products of this process–make up a story to mask the illusory character of what's happened.

When Hume finished explaining what he meant by his claim that there is no self in experience, he appealed to his own experience to verify his claim. He wrote:

> *For my part, when I enter most intimately into what I call myself,*
> *I always stumble on some particular perception or other, of heat or*
> *cold, light or shade, love or hatred, pain or pleasure. I never can*
> *catch myself at any time without a perception, and never can*
> *observe any thing but the perception.*

Then he appealed to the reader's experience:

> *If any one upon serious and unprejudic'd reflection, thinks he has*
> *a different notion of himself, I must confess that I can reason no*
> *longer with him. All I can allow him is, that he may be in the right*
> *as well as I, and that we are essentially different in this particular.*
> *He may perhaps, perceive something simple and continu'd, which*
> *he calls himself; tho' I am certain there is no such principle in me.*[5]

Strictly speaking, Hume denied only that when one introspects one will find a certain sort of datum in experience–"something simple and continu'd," which one calls *oneself.* He did not deny that when one introspects, one discovers the illusion of a self in experience. But neither did he describe an illusion of self in experience.

Many readers of Hume have accepted his invitation to examine their own experience, and have come away from their examinations convinced that he was right–that there is no self in experience. However, one of the great ironies of western philosophy is that as a consequence of Hume's not having gone on to characterize an illusion of self in experience, many of these same readers have failed to notice that an illusion of self was actually an ingredient phenomenologically in the very experiences in which they looked for a self and failed to find one.

Thus, although Hume and Krishnamurti had similar views of the self, there are some interesting differences between them. One of these differences is that Krishnamurti described an illusion of self. Another is that Krishnamurti stressed that the division in experience between observer and observed is a feature even of experiences in which one looks introspectively for the observer. Finally, the objectives of Hume and Krishnamurti in presenting their views were radically different: Hume's was to formulate a correct theory, Krishnamurti's to help his audiences free themselves form the illusion of self.

Failure to appreciate the significance of these differences, particularly on the part of students of western philosophy, may encourage them to think that they understand Krishnamurti when they do not. Most important, perhaps, is that those philosophers and students of western philosophy who have agreed with Hume that there is no permanent self in experience, presumably retained in their experience the illusion of self, often without realizing it, even in the very experiences in which they searched for and failed to find any sort of experiential indication of a permanent self.

Why haven't western philosophers tried to describe the illusion of self in experience? The reason for their neglect is not that illusions in general cannot be described–think, for instance, of the straight stick which, half in water and half out, appears to be bent, and of the phantom limb phenomenon. And it cannot be that the illusion of self is too unimportant to be worth the time and energy it would have taken to describe it. Prima facie this particular illusion is intimately connected with some of our most significant character traits and emotions–with pride and fear of death, for instance–about which philosophers have had a lot to say.

Why, then, have philosophers not paused to describe the illusion of self? The answer, I think, is that they haven't seen it. That is, since they did not recognize that they retained the illusion of self in the very experiences in which they looked for and failed to find a self, they never–or almost never–went on to characterize the illusion of self in experience Their assumption has been that as soon as one searches introspectively for the illusion of self, the illusion dissipates.

The analytic philosopher, Richard Taylor, is a case in point. In a widely read textbook, he expressed what seems to have been (and may still be) a common attitude. He said that we can know that there is no experience of self because we can always say informatively what experiences are like, including illusory experiences, but we can never say informatively what the experience of self is like:

> *One imagines that he is deeply, perpetually, unavoidably aware of something he calls "I" or "me." ... [But] as soon as one begins to try saying anything whatever about this inner self, this central reality, he finds he can say nothing at all. It seems to elude all description. All one can do, apparently, is refer to it; one can never say what is referred to, except by multiplying synonyms–as if the piling of names upon names would somehow guarantee the reality of the thing named! But as soon as even the least description is attempted, one finds that what is described is indistinguishable from absolute nothingness.*[6]

What, then, in the view of someone like Taylor, should we say about those people who think, as many do, that they can introspectively experience a self? Presumably, we should say that they are merely imagining that they can have such an experience. But how could they make a mistake about what they are experiencing? Presumably, they could err by reading too much into their experiences–that is, by confusing an interpretation (or theory) of their own experiences with the experiences themselves. In other words, they may be misled by theories or presuppositions, perhaps derived from common sense, that they bring to their experiences. They may be misled by these theories or presuppositions into thinking that they experience something that they do not actually experience.

In Krishnamurti's view, by contrast, there is an illusion of self in experience, and it does not dissipate as soon as one searches for it introspectively. The illusion is much more stubbornly entrenched in our psyches than that. It enters the mind as soon as we start to conceptualize what we are perceiving, that is, as soon as we form an image:

> *I observe that red-tailed hawk flying by. I see it. when I observe that bird, am I observing with the image I have about that bird, or am I merely observing? . . . If there is an image, which is words, memory and all the rest of it, then there is an observer watching the bird go by. If there is only observation, then there is no observer* (27 Mar 71).

As we have seen, in trying to describe the illusion of self, Krishnamurti said that it shows up primarily as an apparent distinction between "the observer and the observed," which in turn shows up as a kind of "psychological space." So, if he is right, then it turns out that Taylor and like-minded philosophers are wrong: one can say something informative about the illusion of self.

If Krishnamurti were the only one to have noticed the illusion of self in experience, and the way in which it gives rise to the observer/observed distinction, then his view might be suspect. But he is not the only one. In Asian traditions, especially in Indian traditions, there is a long history of meditative reports that support Krishnamurti's characterization of the self. In classical Theravada Buddhist texts, for instance, shedding what Krishnamurti has called the observer/observed distinction is called, "dispelling the illusion of compactness."[7] Jack Engler, a contemporary Buddhist, nicely describes the process:

> *My sense of being an independent observer disappears. The normal sense that I am a fixed, continuous point of observation from which*

I regard now this object, now that, is dispelled. Like the tachistoscopic flicker-fusion phenomenon which produces the illusion of an "object" when discrete and discontinuous images are flashed too quickly for normal perception to distinguish them, my sense of being a separate observer or experiencer behind my observation or experience is revealed to be the result of a perceptual illusion, of my not being normally able to perceive a more microscopic level of events. When my attention is sufficiently refined through training and kept bare of secondary reactions and elaboration of stimuli, all that is actually apparent to me from moment to moment is a mental or physical event and an awareness of that event. In each moment there is simply a process of knowing (nama) and its object (rupa). Each arises separately and simultaneously in each moment of awareness. No enduring or substantial entity or observer or experiencer or angesn–no self–can be found behind or apart from these moment-to-moment events to which they could be attributed (an-atta = no-self). In other words, the individual "frames" appear which had previously fused in normal perception in a tachistoscopic manner to produce an apparently solid and fixed image of a "self" or an "object." The only observable reality at this level is the flow of mental and physical events themselves. There is no awareness of an observer. There are just individual moments of observation.[8]

For a contemporary western audience, this is one of the most phenomenologically precise descriptions of which I'm aware of what shedding the observer/observed distinction in a state of heightened sensitivity, as opposed to a state of concentration or absorption, would involve. Charlotte Jocko Beck, a contemporary commentator on Zen, has made much the same point more informally, by remarking that while it certainly "*looks*" to each of us as though we are "separate from other people and from all else in the phenomenal world," which she says is a source of "much misery," what "we call the self is no more than a series of thoughts" to which "we're attached."[9]

Returning now to the comparison between Hume and Krishnamurti, even though Hume's views have been around for centuries and the Buddha's similar views have been around for millennia, and even though the views of Hume or the Buddha have been understood intellectually by millions of people, that does not mean that millions have ended the illusion of self. According to Krishnamurti, understanding in the relevant way his dictum, "The observer *is* the observed," is a rare achievement. Those who fully understand his dictum end–at least temporarily–the illusion of self as an ingredient of their "experience."[10]

So far as the objectives of Hume and Krishnamurti are concerned, for present purposes, as I mentioned briefly, the main difference between them that matters is that whereas Hume put forth his view as a theory to which he is trying to win intellectual assent, Krishnamurti put forth his as an invitation to see through the illusion of self and thereby end it. Since Hume was after intellectual assent, he would have taken himself to be understood by anyone who could have understood his theory, and his arguments for it, intellectually. One could have shown that one had this kind of understanding by formulating a good objection to his views or by properly relating what he had to say to the theories of someone else. In short, one can understand Hume perfectly, for his purposes, without ending the experiential illusion of self. In fact, to his credit, one of the things Hume seems to have understood is that understanding his view intellectually does not, in fact, end the experiential illusion of self.

Krishnamurti, on the other hand, would not have taken himself to be understood by someone who merely understood intellectually what he was saying and assented to it. In his view, and for his purposes, intellectual understanding hardly counts as understanding at all. That is partly why, from his point of view, his having presented arguments for his view would have been so beside the point. It would merely have encouraged people who did not understand what he was saying in the relevant way to mistakenly think that they did understand him. That is also partly why Krishnamurti is so unconcerned with whether his listeners assent to his views. If they were to assent to them without ending the illusion of self, then they would not have understood his views in the relevant way, and so would not really even be assenting to them, but only to something that they mistakenly took to be his views. Finally, another reason Krishnamurti did not care whether anyone assented to his views is that he did not think that assenting to them would help them to end the illusion of self.

In addition to describing the illusion of self in experience, Krishnamurti characterized its causes and consequences. He said that the illusion is nourished by the one's desire to expand and control the range of one's experiences and that it strengthens that desire:

> *Experience nearly always forms a hardened center in the mind, as the self, which is a deteriorating factor. . . . We all want greater, wider experience of some kind. We think that pursuit of experience is the right way of life . . . The fundamental desire is for greater sensation—to have the sensation of pleasure extended, made high and permanent, as opposed to the suffering, the dullness, the*

routine and loneliness of our daily lives. So the mind is ever seeking experience, and that experience hardens into a center, and from this center we act. We live and have our being in this center, in this accumulated, hardened experience of the past (25 May 56).

But how does experience contribute to the formation of this "hardened center"?

Krishnamurti said that there is a constant interplay between our seeing objectively and our emotive feelings, our beliefs, and what we think that we know. He also said that there is a constant interplay between our seeing objectively and how we react both to what we see in the light of our feeling, believing, and knowing. We see objectively with our senses–especially our eyes and our sense of touch. We emotively feel, believe, and know largely on the basis of our past experiences. And it is on the basis of the past–"the known"–that we react. Reacting, through a process of conceptualization, or "naming," gives rise to *experience*:

> *When I see you, I react . . .The naming of that reaction is experience. If I do not name that reaction, it is not an experience. Please do watch it. Watch your own responses and what is taking place about you. There is no experience unless there is a naming process going on at the same time. If I do not recognize you, how can I have an experience* (19 Jan 52).

So, when the individual–not "the self," but the organism–reacts to something in the world, or to something internal to itself, it gives a name to that reaction, that is, it categories or conceptualizes it. Krishnamurti is saying that experience arises in the process of, and as a consequence of, that categorization or conceptualization. If the individual were to react without conceptualizing, there would be no experience, even though there would still be a conscious interaction between the individual and his or her internal or external environment. In this interaction the individual would be aware, but no "experience" would have taken place.

Often, Krishnamurti said, in reacting to their own internal states, people react to their mental projections, including their desires to be protected, to have security, to have a teacher, a god, wealth, fame, and so on: "I have projected a desire, which has taken a form, to which I have given a name; to that, I react. It is my projection. It is my naming." In other words, the process of naming one's reaction gives rise to experience, which strengthens the self.

So experience is always strengthening the 'me.' The more you are strengthened, the more entrenched you are in your experience and the more does the self get strengthened. As result of this, you have a certain strength of character, strength of knowledge, of belief, which you put across to other people because you know they are not so clever as you are, and because you have the gift of the pen and you are cunning
(19 Jan 52).

But, according to Krishnamurti, in spite of these worldly benefits, ultimately the activity of seeking ever widening experience, because it hardens the self, is destructive.

Suppose that not only understanding intellectually, but seeing in the relevant way all of that, and also seeing how destructive the process of strengthening the self can be, one decides to take a "spiritual" route and opt out altogether from the process of accumulating experiences:

When I desire silence of the mind, what is taking place? What happens? I see the importance of having a silent mind, a quiet mind, for various reasons. I want to have a silent mind, and so I ask you how to get it. I know what this book or that book says about meditation and the various forms of discipline. I want a silent mind through discipline and I experience silence. The self, the "me," has established itself in the experience of silence. Am I making myself clear? (19 Jan 52).

So, in Krishnamurti's view, in one's seeking a silent mind, the very process of seeking insures that one will not attain one's goal. Instead of solving the problem that led to the creation of experience, one has simply replicated the problem in another dimension of experience. That is why, in his view, self-improvement programs, including disciplined meditation practices of whatever sort, are fruitless.

It doesn't get better if one has so-called lofty desires:

I want to understand what is truth; that is my desire, my longing; then there is my projection of what I consider to be the truth, because I have read lots about it; I have heard many people talk about it; religious scriptures have described it. I want all that. What happens? The very want, the very desire is projected and I experience because I recognize that state. If I do not recognize that state, that act, that truth, I would not call it truth. I recognize it and

34

I experience it. That experience gives strength to the self, to the "me" (19 Jan 52).

It may seem, then, that in Krishnamurti's view, we are stuck–tethered to psychologies that are not only destructive, but almost ideally designed to retain their grip on us. For no matter what we want, even if we want to be unstuck, we merely strengthen what binds us.

Is there a super-self, behind the mundane illusory self? In Krishnamurti's view, no. But who then learns that the mundane self is an illusion? Krishnamurti's answer is that no one learns it–that is, there is no *self* that learns it. Rather, the learning is simply revealed in awareness:

> *Awareness has revealed the different states of one's mind, has revealed the various images and the contradiction between the images, has revealed the resulting conflict and the despair at not being able to do anything about it and the various attempts to escape from it. All this has been revealed through cautious hesitant awareness, and then comes the awareness that the observer is the observed. It is not a superior entity who becomes aware of this, it is not a higher self (the superior entity, the higher self, are merely inventions, further images); it is the awareness itself which had revealed that the observer is the observed.* [11]

But if one's awareness is contaminated by thought, then it is incapable of revealing that the observer is the observed. And "if in that state of awareness there is still an entity who says, 'I must be aware, I must practice awareness,' that again is another image."

In Krishnamurti's view, the conceptualization of our reactions to the external world and to our internal states–the conversion of those reactions into "experience"–is not inevitable. By contrast, the vast majority of contemporary philosophers, of all persuasions, think that it is inevitable–that is, that an unconceptualized state of awareness, say, of an external object, is impossible. Among analytic philosophers, for instance, it is widely held that there is no such thing as an "uninterpreted sense-datum." So also among postmodernists. And, in Deconstruction, where the word *text* is used to convey interpretation, Derrida's pronouncement, "Il n'y a pas de hors-texte" ["There is nothing outside the text."] is practically an article of faith. In contrast to all of these philosophers and philosophies, Krishnamurti's view is that there is indeed something outside of the text, and that one can have unmediated, unconceptualized access to it; outside the text is "what is"–reality. That is, in his view, one can perceive reality without conceptualizing what one perceives.

So, who is right–is there such a thing as unconceptualized perception? Traditionally, in philosophy, that question has arisen most often in discussions of mysticism. Throughout time, many mystics have claimed that in "mystical experience" the perception of God, or the One, is not mediated by any concepts–indeed, that its being unmediated is what makes it mystical. It's important to realize that Krishnamurti is saying something more mundane. He is saying that in the perception of *anything*, there is *first* the perception, and *then* the application of concepts (names), and that if one looks carefully one can observe this process.

Going into the philosophy of this issue adequately would take us far afield, in fact into the heart of some of the most difficult issues in contemporary philosophy of mind. Yet, there is a simple exercise you can perform that would *suggest* (not show) that Krishnamurti might be right about this–that is, that it may be possible to have unconceptualized perception. Here is the exercise: In plain daylight, take an ordinary, uncooked egg, smash it eye-level against a white wall, and then watch it drip down the wall. Describe what you see–that is, put your experience into words, conceptualize it, "name" it. Do this as fully as you can. Then ask yourself this: does your description fully capture your experience, or is your experience richer than your description? That is, are there aspects of what you are seeing that go beyond what you have put into words? I think that most of us would say that if we performed the exercise, the experience would be richer than the description. The reason for this is that language merely captures certain gross features of experience, not all of them. Experience is much richer than any language-based set of categories.

But if what we experience in watching the egg drip down the wall is much richer than what we can put into words, that suggests that in perceiving, either we have access to concepts that are not reflected in any natural language and are infinitely more refined than the ones that are so reflected, or else that large parts of our perceptual experience, which nevertheless are perfectly intelligible as perceptions, are unconceptualized. So far as I am aware, there is no reason to believe that we have access to an infinitely more refined array of concepts than are reflected in any natural language. So, it would seem that in perceiving, large parts of our perceptual experience, which nevertheless are perfectly intelligible as perceptions, are unconceptualized. But this claim would seem to be an important part of what Krishnamurti has claimed and many contemporary philosophers have denied. Most of the rest of what Krishnamurti has claimed is that in the process of conceptualization, that is, "naming," unconceptualized perception is transformed into "experience," which thereby strengthens the self.

So, it may be that even in ordinary everyday perception, part of what we perceive is unconceptualized. Could all of what be perceive be left unconceptualized? That is, is the process of conceptualizing our perceptions, and thus strengthening the self avoidable? Krishnamurti thought that it is avoidable. He asked, "Is it possible to live in this world without forming this center," and answered, "I think it is possible." Under what conditions might it be possible?

Only when there is a full awareness of life–an awareness in which there is no motive or choice, but simple observation. I think you will find, if you will experiment with this and think about it a little deeply, that such awareness does not form a center around which experience and the reactions to experience can accumulate. . . . If we can understand this really deeply–that a mind which seeks experience limits itself and is its own source of misery–then perhaps we can find out what it is to be aware. . . . To be aware is to observe–just to observe–without any self-identifying process. Such a mind is free of that hard core which is formed by self-centered activities (19 Jan 52).

So, Krishnamurti has claimed that the process of conceptualizing our perceptions, and thus strengthening the self, is avoidable. It is hard to know whether his claim is true. We have his word for it, although he doesn't want us to take his word for it. Otherwise, except for the equally uncheckable reports of other extraordinary people, we don't have much evidence that the claim is true. But neither, as far as I know, do we have any evidence against it. Perhaps the most we can say is that Krishnamurti's claim could be true, and that if it were true, it would have profound philosophical implications.

What implications? For one, it would imply that ordinary perception is a multi-stage process that begins with an uninterpreted, since unconceptualized, encounter with the world. Thus, when it comes to perception, it is not, as they say, "interpretation all of the way down." Rather, it is interpretation only some of the way down. Beneath interpretation there is *within awareness* an uninterpreted connection with reality. If this is correct, then it means that in the age old philosophical battle between so-called realists and idealists over the nature of perception, the realists would win.

In Krishnamurti's view, of course, there is much more at stake than who wins a philosophical debate. His project is to facilitate people in freeing their minds: "Whatever the mind creates is in a circle, within the field of the self. When the mind is not creating, there is creation, which is not a recognizable process"; "Reality, truth, is not to be recognized. For truth to come, belief, knowledge, experiencing, virtue, pursuit of virtue–which is different from being virtuous–all this must go" (19 Jan 52). And, in his view, all this can go: "If we can think about this, if we can listen to what is being said and at the same time be aware of our own intimations regarding the implications of identification, then I think we shall discover, if we are at all serious, that it is possible to live in this world without the nightmare of identification and the ceaseless struggle to achieve a result" (6 Sept 56).

But what, then, is supposed to take place when in one's awareness it is clear that the observer is the observed? What happens, Krishnamurti said, is that "all action that is the outcome of reaction to like and dislike" comes to an end and the individual–you– discovers "that there is an awareness that has become tremendously alive." It has become alive since "it is not bound to any central issue or to any image–and from that intensity of awareness there is a different quality of attention and therefore [of] the mind–because the mind is this awareness has become extraordinarily sensitive and highly intelligent."[12]

Like Hume, Krishnamurti said that the illusion of self in experience is also the illusion of permanence. The consequences, he thought, are momentous.

If we deeply experienced and understood that the self is very impermanent, then there would be no identification with any particular form of craving, with any particular country, nation, or which any organized system of thought or religion, for with identification comes the horror of war, the ruthlessness of so-called civilization (7 Apr 46).

This is a very heavy claim, so we should try to get as clear about it as we can.

Krishnamurti is saying that the illusion of a permanent self is at the basis of our entire psychological make-up, which in turn is the cause of humanity's most destructive tendencies. If we deeply experienced and understood that the self is impermanent, he claimed, then our lives would be radically, not just marginally, different. We would not identify, and in not identifying we would not think of ideas, values, nations, religions, philosophies, or material possessions as *our own*. The whole fabric of our desires–our "craving"–would change; and some of the worst manifestations of human inhumanity– cruelties of every sort, including war–would cease. Since he believed this, it is no wonder that he regarded conventional philosophizing as a waste of precious time. Conventional philosophizing, even about the self–even about the illusion of self–does not cause the illusion to cease. And, in his view, a great deal hinges on whether the illusion does in fact cease.

Once the illusion of self has come into existence, Krishnamurti claimed, the individual in whose mind the illusion has taken residence is thereby motivated to exert effort on behalf of the self. This effort then further strengthens the illusion of self: "I do not know if you have noticed the constant effort that one is consciously or unconsciously making to express oneself, to be something, either socially, morally, or economically"; "Our whole life is based on the everlasting struggle to arrive, to achieve, to become. The more we struggle, the more significant and exaggerated the self becomes, with all its limitations, fears, ambitions, frustrations." It is then, in Krishnamurti's view, a vicious circle: once the self is in place, self-interested desires arrive, such as the desire "to be somebody"; we exert effort to satisfy these desires, which further strengthens the self, which then gives rise to more self-interested desires, and so on.

According to Krishnamurti what the self seems to observe or perceive is either other contents of the individual's own mind whose self it is or else something in the external world. Since so much of what the individual whose self it is, perceives is laden with his or her own interpretations, a great deal of what one actually perceives are one's own "images." Krishnamurti said that when one person perceives another, the relationship is not between persons but between images, and hence the relationship is not "real."

In sum, in Krishnamurti's view, there arises in the mind an illusory division between part of its contents, which are mistakenly thought to be a permanent perceiver, and other of its contents, which are mistakenly thought to be the objects of this perceiver's perceptions. In reality, the mind includes just the transient mental contents–"images." In the field of these contents of experience, there is no perceiver and nothing is permanent: "The observer *is* the observed."

1. *Woman* is a less complex concept than *wife* since in order to be a wife one has to be a woman, but not vice versa.

2. *Freedom from the Known*, New York: Harper & Row, 1969, p. 96.

3. *Freedom from the Known*, p. 96.

4. *Freedom from the Known*, p. 96.

5. *A Treatise of Human Nature*, L.A. Selby-Bigge (ed.). Oxford: Clarendon Press, 1888 (originally published, 1739), Bk. I, Pt. IV, Sec. VI.

6. *Metaphysics,* 2nd Ed., Prentice-Hall, 1963, p. 124. But contrast the more recent views of Antonio Damasio and Thomas Metzinger in Thomas Metzinger, ed., *Neural Correlates of Consciousness: Empirical and Conceptual Questions*, Cambridge: MIT, 2000, pp. 111-120, 285-306.

7. See, for instance, Vajiranana, P., *Buddhist Meditation in Theory and Practice*. Lumpur: Buddhist Missionary Society, 1975; and B. Nyanamoli, ed. & trans, *Visuddhimagga: The Path of Purification by Buddhaghosha*. 2 vols. Boulder: Shambhala, 1976.

8. Jack Engler, Therapeutic Aims in Psychotherapy and Meditation, pp. 17-52, in K. Wilber, J. Engler, and D.P. Brown, eds., *Transformations of Consciousness,* Boston: Shambhala, 1986, pp. 41-42

9. Charlotte Joko Beck, *Nothing Special,* SanFrancisco: Harper SanFrancisco, 1993, pp. 75, 78.

10. Another difference in the views of Hume and Krishnamurti is that whereas Hume takes perceptions–his analogue to Krishnamurti's minimal "images"–to be primitive, unanalyzable experiential data, Krishnamurti has a view about what gives rise to perceptions/images, the whole field of which he calls, *experience.*

11. *Freedom from the Known*, p. 97.

12. *Freedom from the Known*, p. 98.

5

Identification

Krishnamurti repeatedly stressed the importance of identification in the formation and maintenance of the self. For instance:

The self perpetuates through identification; "My son, my wife, my house, my furniture, my troubles, my anxieties, me and all the rest of it"; the identification with something perpetuates the "me" (19 Nov 70).

The whole process of identification—my house, my name, my possessions, what I will be, the success, the power, the position, the prestige, the identification process is the essence of the self.... (23 June 78).

Identification is the root of the self, with thought and all the rest of it. That is an absolute fact, like a cobra, like a dangerous animal, like a precipice, like taking deadly poison. . . . When . . . identification is absolutely cut out of one's life, there is no callousness then—because that is real (23 June 78).

He talked about how incessant identification is:

If you are aware, you will realize that your mind is constantly engaged in the activities of the ego and its identification (6 Sept 56).

He talked often, though not ever at much length, about identification itself:

> *Can I attend so completely that there is only the act of listening and nothing else, no identification, no saying, yes, that is a good idea, bad idea, that's true, that's false, which are all processes of identification?* (23 June 78)

And, in addition to linking identification with the self, he linked it with other things, such as thought:

> *Thought has a place . . . . When I have to catch a train, when I have to go to the dentist, when I go to do something, [but] it has no place psychologically when there is the identifying process taking place . . . . Identification has made thought do the wrong things. Otherwise thought has its place . . . .* (6 Sept 56).

And such as effort:

> *Effort is the very essence of the self . . . . The maker of the effort . . . has already identified with something greater and is making an effort to reach it* (23 June 78).

Finally, he talked about ending identification:

> *The mind [can] come to a state in which there is no identification at all, and therefore no effort to be something; then there is the cessation of the self, and I think that is the real* (6 Sept 56).

> *The self is non-existent [when] there is no identification of any kind. This is a tremendous thing. Non-identification with anything, with experience, with belief, with a country, with ideas, with ideals, wife, husband, love, no identification at all* (23 June 78).

As these remarks illustrate, Krishnamurti took identification seriously. As they also illustrate, he regarded it as extremely destructive. Within the field of thought, he said, it is identification that first gives rise to the self, it is identification that sustains the self, and when identification ceases, the self ceases. In sum, in his view, there is a mental activity–identification; there is a product of that activity–the self; and there are various consequences of there being a self, and hence indirectly of there being that activity. Some of these consequences are internal to the individual, some of them are external, but virtually all of them are harmful.

When one ceases to identify, in Krishnamurti's view, then the illusion of a distinction in experience between observer and observed also ceases. When that illusion ceases, then one becomes aware in the relevant way that "the observer *is* the observed"; that is, then there is in awareness no observer, just the observed. But, Krishnamurti was careful to point out, the awareness that the observer is the observed is *not* identification with the observed. Rather, the awareness that the observer is the observed is a unification of awareness in which there is no longer any seeming distinction between observer and observed–no longer any psychological space:

> *In ancient China before an artist began to paint anything–a tree, for instance–he would sit down in front of it for days, months, years, it didn't matter how long, until he was the tree. He did not identify himself with the tree, but he was the tree. This means that there was no space between him and the tree, no space between the observer and the observed, no experiencer experiencing the beauty, the movement, the shadow, the depth of a leaf, the quality of color. He was totally the tree, and in that state only could he paint.*[1]

In other words, in the process of identification there is still the phenomenological illusion of an observer, and with it the illusion of psychological space between observer and observed. In a state of awareness in which there is no phenomenological illusion of an observer, there is no such psychological space. It is in that sense that the Chinese artist *was* the tree. It is not that physically there was no distinction between him and the tree. Obviously there was. It is, rather, that phenomenologically there was no illusion that he *as an observer* was separate from the tree *as something observed*.

Although Krishnamurti had quite a bit to say about why people identify, and about the consequences of their identifying, given the importance that he assigned to identification, he had surprisingly little to say about the nature of identification itself–what it actually is, or involves. In his many remarks on the topic, instead of giving a definition of *identification,* or explaining its nature, or giving a psychological analysis of it, he gave examples of it: "my house, my name, my possessions," "good idea, bad idea, that's true, that's false," and so on. I shall return to this issue. One thing Krishnamurti did say about identification is that the reason people identify in the first place is to try to create something permanent internally amid all the impermanence that they perceive: "As the self is in constant flux, we seek, through identification, permanency; identification brings about the illusion of permanency, and it is the loss of this which causes fear"; "We recognize that the self is in constant flux, yet we cling to something which we call the permanent in the self–an enduring self which we fabricate out of the impermanent self" (6 Sept 56). So, in Krishnamurti's view, in response to the perception that they do not have a permanent self, people identify in order to create one. But the effort to create a permanent self is futile. Identification results only in the experiential illusion of a permanent self. According to Krishnamurti, once that illusion is in place in one's mind, it generates fear. For if the illusion were to go away, one would be brought "face to face" once again with one's impermanence. So, we–people–continue to identify largely in response to this continuing fear.

For the purposes of philosophy, it is a pity that Krishnamurti did not go on to say more than this about identification. There are questions that, so far as I know, he never addressed, the answers to which would have clarified his view: Why does an individual who does not yet have a self fear impermanency? At what point in the process of human development does a person acquire a self? Do all humans acquire a self in the same way? Do individual humans in the process of development acquire a self all at once, or gradually? If gradually, are there discrete developmental stages in the acquisition of a self? So far as the illusion of a self in one's experience is concerned, how do normal humans compare with animals? How do normal humans compare with humans who have various kinds of brain injuries or abnormalities that seem to affect their sense of self? And so on. I have no idea whether Krishnamurti had answers to any of these questions. Perhaps he had answers to some of them, but didn't express them because he didn't want to theorize.

In any case, it is clear that in Krishnamurti's saying that people are afraid of abandoning the illusion of their own permanency, he is not saying that they are afraid of abandoning this illusion intellectually. Many philosophers have acknowledged intellectually that there is in their own experience no sign of a permanent self. As many of us know from our own experience, making this acknowledgment does not require any great confrontation with one's deepest fears. In the 6th century B.C.E., the Buddha pointed out that there is in experience no permanent self, and subsequently many students of his thought have *readily* agreed. In the 18th century, David Hume made the same point, and subsequently many have *readily* agreed with him. But one's agreeing intellectually that there is no permanent self in one's experience is not the same as ending the phenomenological illusion of self. In Krishnamurti's view, these two are completely different. His concern is only with the latter–with ending the illusion. His claim is that the prospect of ending it, however dimly this prospect is perceived, causes fear–not a relatively trivial fear, as one might experience in parachuting for the first time out of an airplane, but a deep, existential fear, perhaps the deepest.

As we have seen, although Krishnamurti encouraged people to examine identification, he said relatively little about what identification actually is. So, what would we discover about what identification is, if we took him up on his suggestion that we examine it? I want in the rest of this chapter to address this question. Since Krishnamurti did not himself address it, addressing it will require departing from mere exposition of his thought. Nevertheless, departing in this way, on this topic, will, I think, reveal how what Krishnamurti claimed about the processes of self-constitution is continuous with conventional philosophical theorizing about self-constitution. It will also reveal, I believe, how his approach to the phenomenon of identification, which is rooted in meditation. and the approach of philosophy, which is rooted in intellectual theory, rather than competing with each other, are complementary.

So, what is identification? Obviously, it is a psychological act or process. But there are different kinds of identification. So, identification must involve different kinds of psychological acts or processes. These different kinds of identification may turn out to be fundamentally similar, but they cannot be the same or they would be one, not many. So, for instance, from the point of view of philosophical theory, perhaps the most fundamental difference among kinds of identification is that each of us distinguishes, in our own case, between what's *me* and what's *mine*. The distinction is between what we *are*–"me"–and what we *own*–"mine." Most people suppose what they *are* is their bodies and minds. Their possessions–say, their cars and computers–they merely own; these are not part of what they are.

However, some people, including some famous philosophers, have maintained that peoples' bodies are also their possessions, and hence that people are not even their bodies. Bishop Joseph Butler, an 18th century British moral psychologist, held this view. According to him, it is as if our bodies were artifacts–as if, in relation to our bodies, we were pilots in a ship. "We see with our eyes," he said, "only in the same manner as we do with glasses." He also said, "Upon the whole, then, our organs of sense and our limbs are certainly instruments, which the living persons, ourselves, make use of to perceive and move with: there is not any probability, that they are any more; nor consequently, that we have any other kind of relation to them, than what we may have to any other foreign matter formed into instruments of perception and motion,

45

suppose into a microscope of a staff."[2]

Other philosophers, such as the late 19th century American philosopher, William James, had the opposite view. James maintained that we *are* not only our bodies, but our possessions–for instance, our clothes and furniture. That is, he maintained that our possessions are actually part of ourselves. He said that in the widest sense of the word *self*:

> *A man's Self is the sum total of all that he CAN call his, not only his body and his psychic powers, but his clothes and his house, his wife and children, his ancestors and friends, his reputation and works, his lands and horses, and yacht and bank-account. All these things give him the same emotions. If they wax and prosper, he feels triumphant; if they dwindle and die away, he feels cast down,–not necessarily in the same degree for each thing, but in much the same way for all.*[3]

But surely neither of these views–Butler's or James'–is entirely satisfactory.

Contrary to Butler, we do not possess our bodies in *the same way* that we possess our cars. And contrary to James, our possessions–our cars–do not generally give rise to *the very same* emotions in us as our bodies do. For instance, if I somehow were to find out that tomorrow at noon my body were to be blown up by a terrorist's bomb, I would not feel the same way I would feel if I were to find out that my car were to be blown up. And even if, in some unusual case–suppose, say, that I were a professional automobile racer–I were to feel that strongly about my car, I wouldn't feel that strongly about my other possessions. In any case, it is not just a question of *how strongly* ones feels, but of *how* one feels. So, although I may identify both with my body and with my possessions, and even though at some very general level of description the same process of identification may be going on in both cases, in any normal person's mind the distinction between *me* and *mine*, while somewhat vague at places, is secure.

Most people, of course, arrive at many of their most basic views unreflectively, without thinking much or deeply about them. In the case of the me/mine distinction, they simply adopt whatever version of that distinction is prevalent in their cultures. However, of the people who do give the matter enough thought to formulate their own views, some make the distinction primarily on the basis of theory and some primarily on the basis of experience. Bishop Butler, for instance, arrived at his version of the distinction on the basis of theory. He adopted from a Christianized

Platonism that was prevalent in Britain toward the beginning of the 18th century the view that each of us essentially is an immaterial substance. But if that is what we are, he reasoned, then our bodies are not part of us, except perhaps in a manner of speaking. But if our bodies are not part of us, he wondered, then what relationship do we have to our bodies? Well, what's left? We *must* possess our bodies, he reasoned–the answer must be that our bodies are not our selves, but our possessions, like our eyeglasses. Yet even though he subscribed to that view theoretically, or intellectually, presumably in his affective life, he continued for the most part to experience emotions as if he subscribed to the view that his body is not just one of his possessions but, in part, himself.

In most people, the kind of identification directed toward what each of us calls *me* differs from that directed toward what each of us calls *mine*, that is, from that directed toward what each of us owns. Other people or things with which you might identify–your wife, your children, your religion (that is, the social institution)–are neither part of you nor part of what you own, yet they are in some sense still *yours*. If we use the word *possessions* for the things that one actually legally owns, then we need another word for the things with which one identifies, such as one's religion, that one does not actually own. For lack of a better word, let's call the things with which one identifies that one does not actually own one's *accretions*. Using this terminology, then, there are at least three forms of identification: me (self), $mine_p$ (possessions), $mine_a$ (accretions). No doubt there are other forms of identification as well, but for present purposes these three will do.

The point of making these distinctions among kinds of identification is that in giving a psychological analysis of identification, one will want to give a somewhat different account for each different kind of identification. To illustrate what such an account might be like, I'll begin to give one for the first of the kinds of identification that we just distinguished, the kind expressed by,"This is me." However, in connection with this analysis we need to remember that in response to various circumstances, people tend to expand and contract what they take to be their personal borders. For instance, in attempting to deflect having to take responsibility for having blurted out something awful, one might say, "That was the devil speaking through me," when it was actually the person him or herself speaking. Or, in characterizing an automobile accident, one might say, "He smashed into *me*," when what actually happened is that the other guy smashed into one's car, perhaps even into a car that one had merely rented for the day. Psychologists have theorized about the tendencies people have to expand and contract their borders, but I shall not be concerned here either with their theories or with the phenomena their theories are designed to explain.

With respect to kinds of identification expressed by "This is me," at least two are fundamental. One kind binds each of us together as a self *at* a time. The other binds each of us together as a self *over* time. For instance, right now, your identificatory processes probably encourage you to think that your arm (that is, the current state of your arm) and your current sensations are parts of you, but these same processes do not encourage you to think that Lake Michigan is part of you, even if you are in front of Lake Michigan looking at it. Thinking that your arm and sensations are part of *you* is identification *at a time*. Similarly, right now, your identificatory processes probably encourage you to think that certain past things and events were part of you, while others were not, and that certain future things and events will be part of you, while others will not. That identification *over* time.

Focusing now just on identification *over* time, there is a crucial difference between the ways in which each of us identifies with past, present, and future stages of *ourselves*. For instance, with respect to past stages of *yourself*, you *remember having had* certain experiences and having performed certain actions. With respect to current stages of *yourself*, you are *aware of* having certain experiences and performing certain actions now. With respect to future stages of *yourself*, you *anticipate having* certain experiences and performing certain actions. There is also a crucial difference between the ways in which each of us identifies with *ourselves* and the ways in which we identify with anything else. For instance, you don't remember having had *anyone else's* experiences; you are not currently aware of *anyone else's* experiences in the same way that you are aware of your own; and you do not anticipate having *anyone else's* experiences.

To simplify, I want now to consider your identificatory relationships just to your experiences rather than to your actions, and just to your experiences that you imagine will occur in the future, rather than to those that occurred in the past or that are occurring now. In other words, I want to consider just your anticipations of having experiences. I have already suggested that there is a crucial difference between the ways in which each of us anticipates our own future experiences and the ways in which we anticipate anyone else's. The difference is that normally we–that is, the current stages of ourselves–anticipate *having* the experiences that will be had by future stages of ourselves, but we do not anticipate *having* the experiences that will be had by anyone else. In other words, no matter how close we are to someone else, and no matter how much we value their experiences, we do not anticipate *having* their experiences, but at most *that they will have* certain experiences. There is a great gulf psychologically between anticipating *having* an experience and anticipating *that* an experience will occur. When we anticipate *having* an experience we appropriate the imagined experience. When we anticipate *that* an experience will occur we do not appropriate it.

One of the claimed–but controversial–revelations of contemporary philosophical discussions of personal identity is that there are hypothetical situations in which most of us would anticipate having the experiences of people who we do not think are ourselves and who, judged by normal criteria of personal identity, are not ourselves. That is, the claim is that in very special circumstances, we could anticipate *having* the experiences of *others* in pretty much the same ways as we currently anticipate *having* our *own* future experiences.

Typically the examples used to illustrate this phenomenon are hypothetical. Imagine, for instance, that a person were teletransported from Earth to Mars and replicated in the process, so that, dematerialized on Earth, two copies of the person are constructed at the receiving station on Mars. Since the two on Mars would be different people from each other, arguably neither would be the same person as the person on Earth. Yet, it's fairly easy to imagine contexts in which it would be appropriate for the person on Earth to anticipate *having* the experiences of one or the other, or both, of his or her replicas on Mars. If this is so, then the distinction between self and other is not nearly as fundamental a distinction as it is ordinarily supposed to be.[4]

If, as I think, this claimed revelation of contemporary philosophical theory really is a revelation, then the anticipation of having someone's experience in the future is based on something more basic than our application of–and hence more basic than our attachment to–self-concepts. What this means, arguably, is that the kind of identification involved in regarding certain experiences that will occur in the future as one's own is more fundamental than the self. If this is correct, then while identification might be, as Krishnamurti said that it was, necessary for the self, but it would not be sufficient. In other words, identification would be based on something more basic than the application of self concepts. But if this were so, what could this more basic something be?

As suggested above, it could be *appropriation*. That is, when we anticipate having the experiences of someone in the future, it may be that we are appropriating–that is, declaring ownership of–those imagined future experiences. In real life situations, such acts of anticipatory appropriation are virtually always mediated by self-concepts–I anticipate *my* experiences, not anyone else's. Yet, if current developments in personal identity theory are correct, then in certain hypothetical situations

I may anticipate *having* the experiences of someone who I do not believe is myself. The appropriation involved in this latter sort of anticipation is what is left over from the normal anticipation of having an experience of one's own in the future when we delete from what is involved in the normal anticipation the belief that the experience anticipated is one's own. In sum, if these philosophical theories are correct, then in anticipating having someone's experiences, whether one's own or someone else's, there is a kind of appropriation that is an ingredient in the identificatory anticipation that is more basic than the distinction between self and other. Moreover, in full blown identificatory fantasies, such as occur, say, when we identify fully with a character in a novel or movie–and, hence, "lose ourselves" in the fiction– there may be this same kind of appropriation involved, in this case, of a fictional character's experiences.

I realize that all of this theory is a little too compressed. For present purposes, what is important is not so much the finer points of the theory or the reasons one might be drawn to it, as its implications. And the most important of its implications is that the distinction between self and other is not nearly as fundamental a distinction as has traditionally been thought. If this is correct, then our so-called egoistic survival values would, at bottom, not really be egoistic at all; that is, for most of us egoism and expressions of self-interest would be surface phenomena. This result has few, if any, practical implications. But it is important for anyone who wants to get to the bottom of things, especially in understanding the role of identification in the formation of the self. Thus, for those interested in this sort of philosophy, an important project is that of figuring out what are these more primitive forms of identification that underlie self-constitution. This is one of the ways, arguably, in which the interests in identification of Krishnamurti and of contemporary philosophers are continuous–in which they compliment, rather than compete, with each other.

So, how do we appropriate future experiences? In normal cases, where the future experiences appropriated are "our own," it is not by declaring explicitly that the experiences are our own but, rather, by taking ourselves in the future as the focus of our so-called "self-regarding" affective, cognitive, and behavioral dispositions. In other words, there are certain distinctive identificatory dispositions–so-called "self-regarding" identificatory dispositions–that in real life circumstances we actually have toward ourselves in the future and in hypothetical circumstances we have toward appropriate surrogates for ourselves. These are the identificatory dispositions that link us to future stages of ourselves. What, then, are they?

As indicated, they involve three elements: affect, cognitive contextualizing, and behavior. For instance, imagine that someone is anticipating having the experience of winning the Nobel Prize for literature. Normally, in having this anticipation, she would feel pride [affect]; she would narratize her personal history differently and, thereby, change her understanding of the meaning or significance of many aspects of her life [cognitive contextualizing]; and she would change behaviorally in ways that express her anticipation of winning, for instance, she might adopt a grander tone in her professional correspondence or plan her vacations differently [behavior]. Obviously, this list of self-regarding dispositions could be extended. The ways we appropriate the experiences of ourselves in the future are many and subtle. That's for another occasion. The important point, for now, is that acquisition of these sorts of dispositions is what appropriating future experiences *consists in*. That is, ordinarily one appropriates anticipated experiences not by making some sort of explicit claim of ownership, but simply by responding affectively, cognitively, and behaviorally in ways that in normal circumstances are distinctively "self-regarding."[5]

What I'm suggesting, then, is that there is a complex of affect, cognition, and behavior that ordinarily collectively constitutes our appropriating experiences that we anticipate having. In other words, what I'm suggesting is that this sort of identification equals, or is the same thing as, this sort of appropriating; and this sort of appropriating equals, or is the same thing as, affective, cognitive, and behavioral dispositions of the sorts described. The components of this sort of affect/cognition/behavior complex may vary from person to person and with the same person over time. But at any given time, in the life of any given person, there should be a more or less distinctive constellation of such identificatory dispositions that is directed toward his or her anticipated future experiences. And in real life situations, this constellation of identificatory dispositions would not–except in the case of identificatory fantasies–be directed toward the future experiences of anyone who is not oneself. So, that is a crucial element of the ways in which we identify with future stages of ourselves. It is what the anticipation of having experiences *consists in*. It is part of what Krishnamurti suggested that each of us should examine, but then never told us what we would find if we did.

The briefly sketched theory just given of what the anticipation of having experiences consists in is continuous, on the one side, with philosophical theories of self-constitution and, on the other, with what Krishnamurti had to say about identification. Thus, in this case at least, meditative and philosophical approaches to the self, rather than being

51

antagonistic, seem actually to complement each other.

Notes

1. Freedom from the Known, New York: Harper & Row, 1969, pp. 97-98.

2. Joseph Butler, *The Analogy of Religion, Natural and Revealed*, London: Henry G. Bohn, 1852, pp. 89-90. Originally published in 1736.

3. William James, *The Principles of Psychology*, Two Volumes, New York: Henry Holt & Co., Vol 1, 1918, pp. 291-92. Originally published, 1890.

4. For references to philosophical literature in which such issues are discussed, see the note in the Introduction.

5. Why distinctively "*self*-regarding"? To return to our example, whatever the full account of the woman's anticipating having the experience of being presented with the Nobel Prize, if she were normal, her anticipating being presented with the Prize would be quite different from her anticipating anyone else's experience of being presented with it. Further, it would be different not just because her internal perspective on the world and the other person's internal perspectives are different, or just because she and the other person are different people, but for other and more subtle reasons. For instance, so far as affect is concerned, she wouldn't look forward with the same emotion to the experience of her being presented with the Prize as she would to someone else's being presented with it. Even if she and the other person were great friends and she were thrilled that the other person won the Prize, experientially it wouldn't be the same thrill as she would feel if she anticipated that it were she who was going to win it. We don't have a good vocabulary for distinguishing thrills, so it's hard to put into words just how the two thrills would be different. But ordinarily no one is going to confuse the feeling expressed by, "I can't believe that *I* really won the Prize," with that expressed by, "I can't believe that *you* really won it." Of the two feelings, only something like the former feeling would be appropriate to the anticipation of *having* the experience of being presented with the Prize.

6
Psychology

According to Krishnamurti there is something radically wrong with the ways we lead our lives–something that makes our lives heavy and burdensome.

> *Have you ever wondered why it is that as people grow older they seem to lose all joy in life . . . Look at the older faces around you, see how sad most of them are, how careworn . . ., without a smile.*[1]

What's wrong with the ways we lead our lives, he thought, is that we are driven to achieve. The reason we do that, he said, is that we feel inferior, insufficient. So, we strive to get more of something, or to feel more of something, or to become more of something–ultimately, to become somebody. Eventually, this constant struggling wears us down

In Krishnamurti's view, it is ambition, not the sorts of things that we often announce to ourselves and others as our goals, that explains why we do most of the things we do: "Most of our incentives spring from ambitions, from pride, from the desire to be secure or to be well thought of." Of course, in explaining our actions to ourselves, we do not usually say that we act from ambition. Often we dress our motives up by saying that we are trying to achieve some good, or find the right values, or do something that is essentially worthwhile, and so on. "But behind all these words, all these pleasant-sounding phrases, is not the motive–the urge in some form or another–ambition? I want to achieve; I want to arrive; I want to have comfort, to know a certainty of mind in which there is no conflict" (8 Mar 53). So, in Krishnamurti's view, we, humans, are mired in self-deception. We say that we are acting for noble ends, while all the while what is really behind our behavior is something less attractive–our ambition. And beneath our ambition, its other side, is a seething discontent: "Discontent is the striving after "the more," and contentment is the cessation of that struggle."[2]

Krishnamurti asked whether it is possible for the mind, while it is aware, to be completely free of struggle–that is, whether it is possible for it to be free not just momentarily, but always, so that it discovers joy. It is not possible, he claimed, by striving for joy–by trying to cultivate a mind that is free of struggle in order to experience joy. Striving for joy, he said, like striving for anything else, merely introduces more struggle into our lives. It is possible for the mind to be free of struggle, he claimed, but, "you cannot come to contentment without understanding the whole process of 'the more,' and why the mind demands it."[3]

So, in Krishnamurti's view, here is the situation: we are struggling; we want to cease struggling; if we try to cease struggling, we merely perpetuate our struggling. What then can we do? That is, what can we do to cease struggling that would not backfire and augment our struggling? In still other words, what can we do that might be helpful because it does not involve our trying to be something other than what we are?

We could take a pill, perhaps, but that would be an expression of our trying to be something other than what we are. And taking a pill would simply dull the mind and cover up the problem. So, what's left? What's left is that we can observe our struggle, without trying to do anything about it. We can observe it merely to see it, to understand it, in the moment, exactly for what it is.

> *If you observe from moment to moment how the mind gets caught in everlasting struggle–if you just observe the fact without trying to alter it, without trying to force upon the mind a certain state which you call peace–then you will find that the mind spontaneously ceases to struggle; and in that state it can learn enormously. Learning is then not merely the process of gathering information, but a discovery of the extraordinary riches that lie beyond the hope of the mind; and for the mind*
> *that makes this discovery there is joy.[4]*

Krishnamurti thinks that if you watch yourself, you will see yourself struggling "from morning to night, and how your energy is wasted in this struggle." Then, you will try to understand intellectually why you do that. But, even if you succeed in understanding it intellectually, it will not help: "If you merely explain why you struggle, you get lost in explanations and the struggle continues." Alternatively, "if you observe your mind very quietly without giving explanations, if you just let the mind be aware of its own struggle, you will soon find that there comes a state in which there is no struggle at all, but an astonishing watchfulness," in which "there is no sense of the superior and the inferior"–no "big man," no "little man," no teacher. "All those absurdities are gone because the mind is fully awake; and the mind that is fully awake is joyous."[5] What happens to people whose minds are in such a state, Krishnamurti said, is that they cease to think comparatively–to compare themselves with others or with some ideal, to think in terms of "the more." And that, he said, makes all the difference.

Pride

Suppose, for instance, that you are proud of yourself because you have achieved some sort of success. Krishnamurti said that such a feeling of pride will be based on a comparison–you as opposed to others, you in relation to some ideal. The pride, then, becomes a source of pleasure. But what if, in observing that you are proud, you decide that you want to be "humble." Both your pride and your revolve to be humble are based on attachment to the self, on comparisons. It is not that the first is the problem, and the second the solution. Neither is better than the other. Both are equally destructive. So, trying to be humble will not help.

What, then, will help? Ultimately, in Krishnamurti's view, only one thing:

You have to understand the structure of the "I." You have to be aware of your own thinking; you have to observe how you treat your mother and father, your teacher and the servant; you have to be conscious of how you regard those who are above you and those who are below you, those whom you respect and those whom you despise. All this reveals the ways of the "I." Through understanding the ways of the "I," there is freedom from the "I." That is what matters, not just how to be free of pride.[6]

But isn't pride merely a byproduct of ambition and competitiveness? And aren't ambition and competitiveness necessary if people are to progress?

That's what everyone seems to think: "We say that if we have no ambition, if we have no goal, if we have no aim, we are just decaying. This is so deeply rooted in our minds, in our hearts–this thing to achieve, to arrive, to be" (3 Jan 61). But is that right–is it true that without ambition we would stagnate? Not according to Krishnamurti. In his view, ambition is a form of power. It is the desire to be able to do something better than somebody else. It is based on comparing yourself with others or with an idea, and hence it is rooted in discontent. That is why, he said, the ambitious person can never be happy. But even if his analysis were true, wouldn't ambition still be necessary in order to get things done–in order to move ahead, to progress?

Again, in Krishnamurti's view, the answer is, no. And the reason the answer is, no, he said, is that ambition and interest are two different things, and interest suffices to get things done. If a person is really interested in something–if, say, you really love to paint–then you will paint, and insofar as you merely love to paint you will not be competing to be the best or the most famous painter. Rather, you will simply be expressing your love of painting. "You may be better at painting than I, but I do not compare myself with you. When I paint, I love what I am doing, and for me that is sufficient in itself"(8 Mar 53). So, Krishnamurti thinks that in addition to ambition, there is another motivation to act, and it is one that leads to excellence. This other motivation is love of the activity in which one is involved.

In talking to schoolchildren, Krishnamurti explained what he meant:

When we are seeking a result, the important thing is the result, not the thing we do, in itself. Can we understand and love the thing which we are doing, without caring for what it will produce, what it will get us, or what name or what reputation we will have? Success is an invention of a society which is greedy, which is acquisitive. Can we, each one of us, as we are growing, find out what we really love to do–whether it is mending a shoe, becoming a cobbler, or building a bridge, or being a capable and efficient administrator? Can we have the love of the thing in itself without caring for what it will give us, or what it will do in the world? If we can understand that spirit, that feeling, then, I think, action will not create misery as it does at the present time; then we shall not be in conflict with one another (13 Jan 54).

The difficult thing, he continued, is discovering what it is that you love to do. And part of the reason that this is difficult is that at any given time we may have many contradictory urges and what we want to do may change over time.

So, what happens? "Gradually, because of our rotten education, you are forced into a particular channel, into a particular groove. So you become a clerk or a lawyer or a mischief-monger; and in that job, you live, you compete; you are ambitious, you struggle" (13 Jan 54). Proper education, he said, would help people to discover when they are young what they really love to do, so that they would not later get stuck in a job doing something that they hate or that bores them. But, instead of encouraging you to find out what you really love to do, people tend to encourage you to become a "success." This sort of encouragement is so constant that we internalize it. Eventually, we ourselves want to be a success.

But this wanting to be a success, Krishnamurti said, rather than a good thing, is actually "very destructive; it disintegrates, it destroys." The "becomer," he said, "is a machine, he will never know what real joy is." In order to know joy, one must see exactly "what one is and let that complexity, that beauty, that ugliness, that corruption act without attempting to become something else."

> *However poor you may be, however empty, however dull, if you can see the thing as it is, then that will begin to transform itself. But a mind occupied in becoming something never understands the being. The understanding of the being of what one is–that brings an extraordinary elation, a release of creative thought, creative life. All the religious books, all our education, all our social, cultural approaches are to achieve, to become something. But that has not created a happy world; it has brought enormous misery. We live with ambition. That is our daily bread. But that bread poisons us, produces in us all kinds of misery, mentally and physically, so that the moment we are thwarted and prevented from carrying out our ambition, we fall ill. But a man who has the inward feeling of doing the thing which he loves, without thinking of an end, without thinking of a result–that man has no frustrations, he has no hindrances, he is the real creator* (13 Jan 54).

But, how can seeing all of that bring about change, unless we work hard for change?

Krishnamurti's answer is that the seeing by itself, provided that it is deep enough, leads directly to change: "The very perception of this conflict, perceiving, seeing the very source of this conflict–not what you should do about it–has its own action." So, the question is, "Do I see it as I see a cobra, that it is poisonous? That is the crux of the whole matter." Because "if I see it, I do not have to do a thing about it" (3 Jan 61).

Anger

Pride is obviously bound up with thoughts of the self. What about other aspects of our psychologies, say, emotions, such as anger? Does the same sort of analysis apply to them. According to Krishnamurti, in the case of anger, one has to distinguish between anger which has a physiological cause and anger which has a psychological cause. Simple anger, he said, "a sudden flare-up which is quickly forgotten," may well have a physiological cause. But there is another sort of anger "that is deliberately built up, that has been brewed and that seeks to hurt and destroy," whose roots go deep into our psychologies. This is the anger that mainly causes problems.

The problems caused by psychological anger derive, in part, he said, from the fact that most of us do not mind being angry, and so we find an excuse for it. "Why should we not be angry when there is ill-treatment of another or of ourselves? So we become righteously angry. We never just say we are angry, and stop there." We invent elaborate explanations for our anger. And that is what facilitates anger's sinking its roots deep into our psychologies: "It is the explanation, the verbalization, whether silent or spoken, that sustains anger, that gives it scope and depth. The explanation, silent or spoken, acts as a shield against the discovery of ourselves as we are."[7]

According to Krishnamurti, anger stored up becomes resentment, the antidote to which is forgiveness. But "the storing up of anger is far more significant than forgiveness." For if anger is not stored up, there is no need for forgiveness. The question, then, is how to be free of anger. The answer will not be by our trying to get rid of it, or by our condemning it. These are all wastes of energy that only increase internal conflict and, in any case, could be put to better use. In Krishnamurti's view, even calling your anger, *anger*, is a waste of energy: "Why do you call it anger? Because previously you have been angry, by naming it as anger, you have emphasized the previous experience" (11 July 63).

The point, rather, according to Krishnamurti, is to see your present anger for the destructive thing that it is—that is, to see not just an angry episode, but the whole structure of your anger for the destructive thing that it is. And to do that, he said, you cannot pass judgment on your anger, for then "you cannot see it as it is." Your expressions of anger may sound terrible—you may scream, "I hate you." But if you resolve, "I must not hate; I must have love in my heart," it will not solve the problem, but only add an additional layer of conflict to an already difficult situation. To solve the problem, you have to understand your anger completely, and that's all. Nothing else is required, for if you "go into it completely, it ceases." In other words, "to live completely, fully, in the moment is to live with *what is*, the actual, without any sense of condemnation or justification—then you understand it so totally that you are finished with it. When you see clearly, the problem is solved."[8]

59

Guilt

What about other aspects of our psychologies, such as guilt? According to Krishnamurti, guilt is "the feeling that you must submit, you must accept, you must obey." It makes you feel lonely and depressed. And if the guilt is strong, you cannot resolve it. So, what to do? As in the case of every other human psychological (as opposed to physiological) problem, the proper approach, he thought, to not try to resolve one's guilt, but to try to understand it.

So why do people–you, for instance–feel guilty, in the first place? In Krishnamurti's view, it is because others–your parents, your teachers, society–have encouraged you to feel that way. And why have they done that? To control you. It is very convenient for them, he said, if you feel guilty. And religion has played a special role in promoting guilt.

> *In Christianity, there is the original sin and the savior, and therefore I must feel guilty–and confession, and the whole circus begins. Forgive me if I use that word. It takes different forms. In the Christian world– confession, absolution. And in the Asiatic world it has a different form: they go to temples–you know, all kinds of things they do* (14 May 85).

But how does the mechanism work? At the root of it, Krishnamurti said, is that we are trained to have problems.

When a child goes to school, he said, first, reading and writing and then other subjects become problems. Others expect children to achieve, and soon they expect themselves to achieve.

> *Go into the mechanism of guilt, its relation to the ego; and we said don't separate the two, because guilt is part of the ego, part of the "me." It's not separate. Therefore it's not something related to. It is in, it is there. Then we said, why do we have problems. Problems exist from childhood, from the child who goes to the school. He is educated to have problems. So his whole life becomes a problem: depression, anxiety, and so on. Then he goes and asks another; which means asking help from another. But the other is himself; the other has problems, gets depressed, feels lonely. So the other is you. I wonder if you realize this. Therefore, what's the good of asking him?*
> (14 May 85)

So, guilt is intertwined with one's basic psychology, with who one thinks one is, and it is a problem that ultimately one will have to resolve by oneself. But how?

First, by realizing that guilt arises out of fragmentation.

If you are living intensely with your whole being, if you are fully aware of everything about you and within yourself, the unconscious as well as the conscious, where is there room for guilt? It is the man who lives in fragments, who is divided within himself, that feels guilty. One part of him is good, the other part corrupt; one part is trying to be noble, and the other is ignoble; one part is ambitious, ruthless, and the other part talks about peace, love (10 Feb 57).

But what all of this has in common is that it is within the pattern of one's own making.

As long as there is self-centered activity, you cannot get over the feeling of guilt, it is impossible. That feeling disappears only when you approach life totally, with your whole being, that is, when there is no self-fulfillment of any kind. then you will find that the sense of guilt does not exist at all because you are not thinking about yourself. There is no self-centered activity (10 Feb 57).

So, that is the connection between guilt and the ego.

Guilt arises out of the past, but how does the past exert influence on the present?

I feel guilt—why do I name it? I name it instantly. The naming of it is the recognition of it, therefore I have had that feeling before. And having had it before, I recognize it now. Through recognition I strengthen what has happened before (1 Aug 73).

It is a process that replicates itself throughout our psychological life:

Every form of recognition strengthens the past. And recognition takes place through naming. So by and through recognition I strengthen the past (1 Aug 73).

And why do we keep doing that?

In Krishnamurti's view, we keep doing it because we are afraid. Of what? Of being aware without our minds being otherwise "occupied." So, driven by this fear we see to it that our minds are "occupied, whether with God, with smoke, with sex," or whatever. Our minds have to be occupied. We are afraid for them not to be occupied. "And in occupation with the feeling of guilt, in that feeling there is a certain security. At least I have that thing; I have nothing else, but at least I have that feeling of guilt" (1 Aug 73).

There arises, then, a basic question: When you begin to feel guilty can you observe the feeling without naming it, without recognizing it as guilt, or for that matter, without recognizing it as anything at all? "So, I find when I do not name, the thing no longer exists. And I am afraid–listen to this carefully–the mind is afraid of living in a state of nothingness. Therefore it has to have a word." And words inevitably function to import the past into the present. "The word–listen to this–the word is the past, the word is the memory, the word is thought" (1 Aug 73). Ultimately, then, thought is the problem.

Notes

1. *Think on These* Things, New York: Harper & Row, 1970, p. 193.

2. *Think on These Things*, p. 196.

3. *Think on These Things*, p. 196.

4. *Think on These Things, p. 195.*

5. *Think on These Things*, p. 195.

6. Commentaries on Living, Series I, Theosophical Publishing House, 1989, p. 70.

7. *Commentaries on Living*, Series I, p. 70.

8. *Freedom from the Known*, New York: Harper & Row, 1969, p. 55.

7
Art of Living

What brings about fragmentation and internal conflict? According to Krishnamurti it is importing the past into the present. This is done by thought. For many purposes, of course, thought is essential. But, in Krishnamurti's view, a huge drawback of thought is that "is never new and can never be new." Life, on the other hand, is "always active, in the present."

> *When you try to understand activity in the present, with the past, which is thought, then you don't understand it at all; then there is fragmentation, and life becomes a conflict. So, can you live so completely that there is only the active present now? And you cannot live that way if you haven't understood and thereby cut yourself off completely from the past, because you yourself are the past* (12 Jan 68).

So, in the last analysis, thought is the problem. Leaving thought behind when it is not needed is the solution. Krishnamurti said, "I think, if you have the energy, the drive, the passion," then leaving thought behind when it is not needed "is the only way to live."

How does one leave thought behind? In Krishnamurti's view, there can be no "how" to it. Even to think in terms of method–of doing one thing in order to secure another–is to come under the dominion of thought, and therefore to guarantee that you will not succeed in leaving thought behind.

That is why effort to achieve an end will not get you where you need to go. What will? In his view, truth–that is, awareness of truth–will.

But what about life's normal array of problems? Fate has dealt many people a poor hand: they were born deformed or unhealthy, or in poverty; where they just happened to be, the volcano erupted, the war broke out, the crops failed, and so on. In the case of those of us who have been more fortunate, it seems that regardless of how good we may have it, we still want more. We harbor schemes to make our lives even better, easier, more pleasurable. And, ironically, if the others who now have it so much worse than most of us have it had it much better–as good as we now have it–they too would want more. So, what to do: about the problems of others, about our own problems, about everyone's chronic lack of fulfillment?

Krishnamurti proposed an analysis of the source not of all human problems, but of those that humans create for themselves–the bombs, the rapes, the abuse, the hopelessness, the secret longings unfulfilled. He proposed a simple, but elusive solution. In his view, human nature is the source of the problems. And to prevent the problems from continuing to arise again and again, human nature has to change.

More specifically, Krishnamurti claimed that unless each of us transforms psychologically so as to remove certain fundamental sources of conflict from our lives, three things will happen: we will lead internally conflicted lives, our internal conflicts will get expressed in our external behavior, and our external behavior will create, or contribute to creating, serious problems for others. On the other hand, he said, if we transform fundamentally in the relevant way, then each of us will live in harmony with ourselves, this harmony will be expressed in our external behavior, and we will thereby help others. In sum, in his view, regardless of what each of us is doing or may do, if we do not transform, then we are, and will remain, part of the problem, but if we do transform, then we become part of the solution.

How, in Krishnamurti's view, did you and I get to be so internally conflicted? His answer, in one word: thought. According to him, the ultimate source of our being so internally conflicted is that we think when we should be mentally still, and in thinking, we identify. What we identify with is either our own thoughts, including especially what we mistakenly take to be our selves, or something outside of our minds–such as an ethnic group, or religion, or nation–that we view through the lens of our thoughts.

Krishnamurti acknowledged, of course, that for many purposes thinking is indispensable. But he claimed that when thinking is employed outside of its proper role, as it often is, it causes problems. Identification, it seems, has no proper role to play. According to him the solution to those problems that are due to thinking when we should be mentally silent, and then to identifying with, or through, our thoughts, is to stop thinking when we should not be thinking and to stop identifying altogether.

But these suggestions of Krishnamurti raise questions: For one thing, on what occasions and for what purposes is thought useful and when is it not useful? That is, what is the proper role of thinking. Krishnamurti often used the expression, "technological," to characterize the sort of thinking that he allowed can be useful. For instance, he said that if you were going to build a bridge, it would be a good idea to consult and then follow sound principles of engineering. But, in his view, thought of various kinds that goes well beyond technology narrowly construed, and perhaps even beyond merely implementing practical tasks, may also be useful.

How far beyond, and what sorts of tasks? From everything that Krishnamurti has said, it is not clear exactly where, or on what basis, he would draw the line between those occasions when–or those uses for which– thought is helpful, and those when–and for which–mental silence would be better. His view seems to have been that a person who cultivates what he called intelligence will know intuitively when and for what purposes to think and when and for what purposes to be silent, and then automatically do the right thing. That may be true, but it is not very informative.

Krishnamurti said that identification is born of our desire for security and that it is a way of enclosing ourselves psychologically, of setting up artificial boundaries. That seems right. However, as we have seen, other than that he said little about what identification is. Since we are said to identify with thoughts, for instance, with a self, identification may not itself be a thought, but rather a mental operation that is performed on thoughts, as well as on other things to which we are related indirectly through the medium of thought. But what sort of mental operation? And if identification is not this, then what is it? In the previous chapter, I suggested a way in which one might begin to pursue this question that would make Krishnamurti's thought continuous with philosophical theorizing. I do not know whether he would have welcomed this way of extending his views. But, if he rejected it, the question would remain: What is identification?

Whatever identification is, Krishnamurti seems to have thought that it has little, if any, useful role to play in our lives. He was convinced that to really solve our problems, and not just put a patch on them, we need to root our problems out at their source. His disapproval of identification and this conviction seems to have been at the basis of his generally negative assessment of any sort of organized political activity. He said, for instance, "If you and I as individuals really put our minds to this, we shall see that change does not come about through ideals, through time, through pressure and convenience, or though any form of political activity, but only through being deeply concerned with bringing about a radical transformation in ourselves" (27Jan57).

It seems to me that if we accept Krishnamurti's invitation to put our minds to this issue, what we shall see is not what Krishnamurti said we would see, but rather that some useful change–in fact, quite a bit of pretty important useful change–has come about through political activity. Freedom of expression, equality before the law, the welfare of children, and the integrity of the environment are much better protected in some parts of the world and at some times, than in others. Their being better protected is a direct consequence of people having organized into groups and then having acted politically. And these changes, while primarily external, have played and still play a role in sensitizing everyone to the importance of the issues to which the changes are addressed.

Since, in Krishnamurti's view, thought, broadly construed to include identification, is the ultimate problem, a central question–perhaps the central question–is that of whether for ordinary people such as you and I, thought can end completely? In other words, on those occasions when thought is not needed to deal intelligently with some situation, can we, while remaining aware, have minds that are still?

Krishnamurti's view was that while remaining aware we can have minds that are still, and that only then can we be in direct relationship mentally with other people and things. So, what is involved in having a mind that is still?

When Krishnamurti talked about ending thought in the context of "cutting ourselves off completely from the past," he may have meant by "thought," just occurrent thoughts, that is, what a person is actively thinking at the time in question, whether consciously or unconsciously, or he may have meant both occurrent and so-called dispositional thoughts, such as one's stored belief, say, that $7 + 5 = 12$. Which did he mean? Pretty clearly, he meant just occurrent thoughts. Not only did he often say things that imply that he meant this, but he could hardly have meant that by ending thought completely one thereby erases from one's brain all of what one has learned from past experience. If one did that, one would regress to the status of a newborn, with no recoverable memories, and one would have to relearn many basic things that one formerly knew, including how to walk and talk.

Krishnamurti acknowledged all of this.

Look, I must have memory in order to go to my house. I must have memory to talk English. I must have memory to come here and sit on this platform. I must have memory for the language that I use. I have memory of riding a bicycle, or driving a car. So, memory is absolutely essential, otherwise I couldn't function. Memory is knowledge, we must have knowledge (1 Aug 73).

But, if the thoughts that are to end completely are only one's occurrent thoughts, then a clearer way to express the question of whether while we remain fully aware, thought can end completely would be whether while we remain fully aware we can cease thinking completely. That seems to be what is required to have a mind that is still. Can we do it?

Perhaps many of us want to have minds that on appropriate occasions are still. And, as Krishnamurti claimed, it may well be that our wanting to have such minds is, in part, an obstacle to our actually having them. Our wanting is an expression of our greed, and greed is part of the problem, which is the past, not, in Krishnamurti's view, part of the solution, which is to leave the past behind completely. Still, if we did not want to have minds that are still, probably we would not even be concerned with meditation or with what Krishnamurti had to say. So, how could that lack of wanting be better?

A possible answer is that through attention, our wanting to have minds that are still may cease to be an occurrent wanting. In other words, our wanting, which is an expression of our identification with the self, may, through giving our total attention to our current experience and behavior, or to some question with which we've been challenged, recede back into our dispositional psychology, like our stored beliefs. And that may be all that is required.

Krishnamurti had a view about what our best response–that is, the best response of the untransformed–would be to the question of whether while remaining aware we can cease thinking completely. In his opinion, our best response would be neither for us to think that we can cease thinking completely nor to think that we cannot cease thinking completely. Rather, our best response would be to admit that we really do not know whether we can cease thinking completely. He gave two reasons why this would be our best response. First, the only way for those of us who are untransformed to know that while remaining fully aware we could cease thinking completely would be to take somebody else's word for it, such as his own word for it. He said that on the basis of what we now know, there is no way for us to tell whether those, such as himself, who say that it is possible while remaining fully aware to cease thinking completely, are telling the truth. Second, if one really does not know whether while remaining fully aware one can cease thinking completely, then one is not waiting for an answer, or expecting an answer, or even wanting an answer. In his view, there is a crucial drawback to being in any of these mental states. It is that if one is in one of these states, then one has not ceased thinking completely, and so one's mind is not still.

Suppose, then, we admit, as it seems to me most of us should anyway, that we really do not know whether while remaining fully aware we can cease thinking completely. Would that admission bring our minds any closer to being still? Krishnamurti said:

We have posed a question. That is, can the rhythm of thought which

68

has been going on from the beginning of one's life until we die, can that rhythm of thought come to an end? You reply and this dialogue goes on. And then . . . in that process only the question remains–right? You don't answer. I don't answer. Now, when the question remains, your brain is quiet, because you are not acting. I am not acting, only the question (12 Jun 84).

My understanding of what Krishnamurti meant by these remarks is that the point of confronting the question of whether while remaining aware we can cease thinking completely is to create a psychological context that facilitates the mind's being still. Dialogue is one way of creating such a facilitating context. However, there are also other ways, such as giving one's complete attention to one's current experience and behavior.

If this interpretation of Krishnamurti is basically right, then, is there a bottom line? And if there is, what is it? I think that there is a bottom line–this: So far as the art of living is concerned, our "project," if we follow Krishnamurti's numerous suggestions, is to do whatever will facilitate being fully aware while our minds are completely still. Ultimately all we can do to facilitate this is just to pay attention totally, but otherwise not to have any occurrent projects. Pay attention to what? To everything that enters into our current experience, but particularly to ourselves in relationship. Why pay attention? Because we will thereby learn the truth about ourselves, or at least truths about ourselves, and truth frees. However, if due to our occurrent wanting, we pay attention in order to be free, then we do not pay attention totally, and so we remain bound. To be free, Krishnamurti said, we must let go of the past completely, including letting go of any occurrent want we may have to be free. In sum, attention, which is without motive, or at least without occurrent motive, leads to truth, which frees.

Bibliography

Works By Krishnamurti

Awakening of Intelligence, San Francisco: HarperSan Francisco, 1987

Education and the Significance of Life, San Francisco: HarperSan Francisco, 1981

Freedom from the Known, New York: Harper & Row, 1969.

The Ending of Time: J. Krishnamurti and David Bohm, San Francisco: HarperSanFrancisco, 1985.

The Impossible Question, New York: Harper & Row, 1972

The Limits of Thought, New York: Routledge, 1999

The Wholeness of Life, San Francisco: Harper & Row, 1979.

The Collected Works of Krishnamurti, 17 vols., Dubuque, Iowa: Kendall Hunt, 1991.

Works On Krishnamurti

Evelyn Blau, *Krishnamurti: 100 Years*, New York: Stewart, Tabori, and Chang, 1995.